I am one who
was ordered by the Nazis to pass through their gates.

I am one who
has seen the smoke coming out of
the crematorium chimneys.

I am one who
has seen the one-way entry into the gas chambers.

I am one who
has smelled the stench from burning bodies.

I am a survivor of the Holocaust.

I am Michael Weiss.

From Kaszony To Auschwitz To Detroit

CHIMNEYS
– AND –
CHAMBERS

The Lingering Smell Of The Holocaust

by

Michael Weiss

Mazo Publishers

Chimneys and Chambers:
The Lingering Smell Of The Holocaust

ISBN 978-1-936778-39-3
Copyright © 2015 by Michael Weiss

Published by

Mazo Publishers
P.O. Box 10474
Jacksonville, FL 32247 USA

www.mazopublishers.com
Email: mazopublishers@gmail.com
Tel: 1-815-301-3559

[3]

In the presence of eyes
Which witnessed the slaughter
Which saw the oppression
The heart could not bear,
We have taken an oath:

To remember it all,
To remember, not once to forget!
Forget not one thing to the last generation!

Avraham Shlonsky

Contents

Preface   8
Acknowledgments   11
Comments From Family And Friends   14

Growing Up In Kaszony   26
Preparing For Passover   36
The Beginning Of The Holocaust   40
Deportation To The Ghetto   48
Auschwitz   56
Buchenwald   59
Zeitz   62
Liberation   66
The United States of America   73
Lilly Weiss Is Also A Survivor   86
A Second Generation Survivor   95
To Remember And Remind   98
Israel – Our Homeland   105
Jerusalem   109
Legacy Of The Survivors   111
Heroes   117
Do Not Forget   121
Events For Remembering   124
Tisha B'Av And The Holocaust   128

Preface

Like many Holocaust survivors, for a long time I avoided discussing the Holocaust and what happened to my family and me during those years. It is difficult for people who did not experience the Holocaust to understand why, for so many years, survivors did not want to talk about their experiences.

During the last 70 years since liberation from the concentration camp, my family and friends always wanted me to write about my experiences in the Holocaust. They wanted me to share what I saw and what I went through. They wanted this information for future generations to have an understanding of what happened to the Jewish people in Europe in the time leading up to and during World War II. From those terrible experiences – from those terrible years in the Holocaust – from Michael Weiss, survivor, they wanted to hear the story.

Michael Weiss.

But for some reason, I did not want to do it. Maybe it was too hard ... Maybe it was too painful to remember it. When I think about what happened to us, to the Jewish people of Europe, what happened to our communities, to our Jewish life ... My memories of the Holocaust are with me night and day.

Then society changed and people started to say the Holocaust never happened. I started to hear that there are professors teaching courses in college today to deny that the Holocaust happened. And I began to hear about people who are writing books saying that the Holocaust never happened. And that people are signing up for the courses, buying the books – and believing.

Let me tell you to never forget or be misled – the Holocaust did happen. I saw it. I felt it. I smelled it.

After liberation, we really found out the terrible tragedy that had befallen us, the Jewish people. By now, most of us survivors are retired with little to do, except to think of those past bitter memories ... what we cannot and will not forget. They are chiseled in our minds – forever.

There were over eight million Jews in Europe during the reign of Nazi terror. The Nazis murdered a million and a half children and another four and half million adults. Six Million. Six Million Jews perished at the hands of the German Nazis.

Not only is the Holocaust a story of the persecuted and the murdered, but it is also a story of defiance and courage. This is my story. I was imprisoned in the concentration camps of Auschwitz and Buchenwald.

We say on Shavuot, in the *Akdumos*, the *Doai Ele Yami* (If all the oceans of the world would be ink, there would not be enough ink to write down the goodness of God). And I say, if all the oceans of the world would be ink, you couldn't write down the tortures, the barbaric, inhumane treatment which was executed against us Jews.

The people of Europe were religious people on Sundays. I heard church bells ringing on Sundays ... people were dressed in their best attire and they were going to church. As I was growing up, they sounded very friendly to us. But, when Hungary occupied Czechoslovakia and joined Hitler, somehow, they all changed, they acted hateful and really meant it ... they agreed they wanted to kill all of the Jewish people. God forbid, they almost succeeded. I recall when the people of Europe took us out of our homes, right after

Passover in 1944, I thought Jewish life stopped right there ...

Hitler wrote in his 1933 book, *Mein Kampf,* he wanted to make Europe "Judenrein" (meaning there shouldn't be a Jew in Europe).   After the war, Europe was Judenrein.

As I have reached the ripe old age of 90, and only a handful of survivors remain alive, I have decided that it is time to tell you this story. It is my duty as an eyewitness to the Nazi atrocities.

I started to write this book after Passover 2015 and today we are after Sukkos 2015, and I have finished my book.

We, the survivors,
WILL remember the Holocaust forever.

We, the Jewish people,
HAVE to remember the Holocaust forever.

Not only the people of Europe, but the
people of the rest of the world too,
MUST remember the Holocaust forever.

Acknowledgments

I would like to say thank you to my family and many dear friends who have helped me in my life and especially with this book.

I will always remember three great Rabbis who have played very important roles in my life. I want to recognize my Rabbi in Kaszony, Harav Yisrael Tzvi Halevi Rottenberg. He was my mohel, (the Rabbi who circumcised me) and later my teacher. He gave me great support and spiritual strength when we were together in Auschwitz.

I remember Rabbi Goldman, whom I met when I came to Detroit. He was my Rabbi and teacher and my friend, along with his wife and children.

In my shul today, Congregation Dovid Ben Nuchim, Rabbi Ari Kostelitz, who is a young Rabbi with a fine family, is a devoted friend and spiritual leader. He is a third generation Holocaust survivor. I hope and pray that he will lead us *Kegen Mashiach*, to welcome the Messiah.

I thank my wife for supporting me in all of my efforts towards this book. In the last six months, it has happened many times, I left home with the kitchen table full of papers! Papers were on the pantry, on top of the washer and dryer ... I would come home and everything would be organized!

With my wife, Lilly.

To our daughter Eva Aron, for her thoughtful and loving additions to the book.

To my son Arthur, from whom, in a way, I took over his office. I never asked if he was busy ... I would just show up!

To my son Mottel, whom I called many times and asked how to finish a sentence, how to write it so it would be understandable.

I would like to thank and acknowledge my many friends who contributed to this book.

Stephen Goldman, Executive Director at the Holocaust Memorial Center's Zekelman Family Campus.

Kenneth Waltzer, Director of the Jewish Studies program at Michigan State University.

Dr. Elliott Weinhouse M.D., Professor of Pediatrics, Pediatric Cardiology at Beaumont Health System in Royal Oak, Michigan.

Charles Silow, PhD, President of C.H.A.I.M. (Children of Holocaust Survivors Association in Michigan).

David Shay for ALL the driving and more importantly, your friendship, which helped me to be on time ALWAYS in the synagogue.

Boruch Rubinfeld for his guidance throughout our services.

Tuvia Nickel for all of the professional pictures you supplied to the publisher, and for all of your help through the years.

Jim MacDonald, who is my son's paralegal, for his invaluable assistance, and during the last six months, always being available to me in order to finish this book. When I would come to the office, I could see that he was busy, but he would take the time I needed and typed, re-typed, and edited my sentences.

I would like to thank Chaim Mazo and the staff at Mazo Publishers for their efforts in putting my book together in a format easily understood by the reader. Although I have not yet had the pleasure of meeting Mr. Mazo in person, we have spoken often on the phone about the book, and we have become very good friends. As a matter of fact, at one point, I talked to him like I would converse with my father ... but thinking it over, I think he's like my "son" or "grandson."

Over the years I have read books by other survivors. I was amazed at how we had so many experiences in our families that were so similar, especially how our mothers prepared their homes for Shabbos and the holidays. And for many of us, the tragic experience in the Holocaust was identical.

Two books stand out and were helpful to me in preparing my story. One is "Not To Forget, Impossible To Forgive" by Dr. Moshe Avital. This book was one of the best books I've seen in the last fifty years! It was also published by Mr. Mazo and his staff. This is one of the reasons why I picked him and his staff to publish my book! The other book is "The Jews Of Kaszony, Subcarpathia" by Joseph Eden.

With love and thankfulness to all,

Michael Weiss

In front of the Aron Kodesh with many of my friends at
Congregation Dovid Ben Nuchim.

Comments From Family And Friends

Arthur Jay Weiss

The son of survivors, born a few years after Liberation, growing up in northwest Detroit of the 1950s, the spectre of the Holocaust approached gradually and poignantly. Through the eyes of an adolescent, recognition of numbers branded onto forearms, the lack of extended family members and the apprehension of Adolf Eichmann created an unsettling image, which, rather than diminish, has intensified over the last six decades.

While the United States was confronted with issues of inequality and foreign wars, survivors endeavored to preserve memories of what had transpired and remain vigilant against re-occurrence. The grandeur of this country was tempered with awareness of a pre-war isolationist policy preventing emigration and, during the war, failure to impede The Final Solution when rumor of the incomprehensible became a grotesque reality.

The endeavors of people such as my father culminated at the First World Gathering of Holocaust Survivors in Jerusalem. The recognition that survivors all over the globe were engaging in activities similar to what my parents and their friends had been doing in Detroit left a profound and lasting effect. A few years later when he retired, lecturing and volunteering at our local Holocaust Memorial Center became his vocation. Often he has spoken of the belief had the war lasted a few more months with conditions being so dire, there would have been no survivors. A resolve to prevent the remnants of Nazism and their proxies from obtaining the victory they were denied seventy years ago has remained steadfast.

The celebration of his fourteenth birthday was supplanted

with the menace of Kristallnacht and what it foreshadowed. He has now written this book as he approaches his ninety-first birthday. My father is acutely aware of pervasive current politics which threaten the existence of Israel and question the propriety of immigrants in this country ... the constant worry of "what if" is haunting.

For us we can only fathom the death and destruction of The Holocaust. My father has committed the majority of his life to prevent those who would have had exterminated our people from claiming victory. What the Nazis sought to deny him – life, family, tradition – he has taken for himself. To paraphrase the Partisan Song, "He is here!"

―❦―

Rabbi Mordechai Weiss

Here, in the Detroit Jewish community, the name of my father, Michael Weiss, is synonymous with Holocaust education. As a volunteer lecturer at the Holocaust Memorial Center and a frequent speaker at his shul, my father has accepted upon himself the mission of telling his story and urging everyone to never forget the atrocities that happened to our people.

Over the years I have implored my father to record his story in book form to educate the public, young and old, and to preserve his legacy for future generations. I am ecstatic to see that his work has come to fruition. I also asked him if I could include my thoughts about being a second generation survivor, and I am honored that he agreed.

During the holiday of Passover, Jewish families around the world gather together to conduct the Passover Seder, read from the Haggadah and recount the story of the exodus from Egypt. It has also been the custom for many survivors to organize events between Passover and Shavuous to remember the six million Jews who died in the Holocaust after Passover. And, as with Passover, families come to gather together to participate, to listen and to recount the events of the Holocaust. The timing is no mere coincidence. On the one hand, the connection between the Haggadah and the Holocaust is incredibly incomprehensible, since Passover is the birth of a people, whereas the Holocaust is the near destruction of that people. But, upon closer examination, both share the similarity of changing the course of our history. And just as there is a special mitzvah to remember the exodus of Egypt which is the birth of our people, so, too, we must remember the days of the Holocaust which is the near annihilation of our people.

We are obligated to remember the story of Passover, because it was that event that gave us our own identity. It made us into a chosen nation, the Jewish people. Without that identity, we are nothing.

The Holocaust is not just a mere historical event that should be thrown into history books. It is something that we must continuously remember and never forget, nor can we ever allow our children to forget. The Holocaust is about us. It happened to us.

The Haggadah teaches us the proper way to remember the exodus. Each person must envision as if he had personally come out of Egypt. But how can we do that? We were not enslaved by Pharaoh. We were not there when Moses led us out of Egypt and wandered through the desert. How can we truly feel and remember something if we were not there? It is for this reason why the Haggadah instructs us to close our eyes and picture ourselves as if we were there. We are obligated to do just that, because if we don't, we simply cannot remember.

However, when survivors gather together to remember the Holocaust they are not obligated to envision as if they were there. They were there! Those who lived through the war saw the concentration camps, the gas chambers, the crematoriums and their family members being tortured and killed. They don't need to pretend they were there. For them, it was reality.

And even for the children of the survivors, the second generation survivors, such as me and my brother, the Holocaust for us was definitely reality; not for what we saw, but for what we didn't see and for what we didn't have.

For many years my family has been treated to something special. When my children were younger, I remember the times we were sitting around the dinner table or relaxing in the den when we would hear the doorbell ring. The children immediately ran to the door. They had a feeling they knew who it was. My wife and I then heard a chorus of jubilant shouts, "Zeidy! It's Zeidy! Zeidy's here!" It was very exciting.

And now that I am blessed with my own grandchildren, it brings me much joy when I come through the door, and my grandchildren run to me and call out, "Zeidy! Zeidy!"

But when I was a child I never said those words. I had no Zeidy. I had no Zeidy to teach me, to encourage me, to hug me, to love me. Hitler took him away. Yes, I know the Holocaust happened, not because I read it in some book, but because it happened to me.

A number of years ago my family traveled to New York to attend a wedding. It was exciting for us, especially for our children. Their first cousin was getting married. They danced at their cousin's wedding. I never had a chance to dance at any of my cousins' weddings. Hitler took them away from me.

Yes, we second generation survivors did not live during the Holocaust, but we definitely did experience the aftermath. And for us, just as for the survivors, we don't have to pretend we were there. We don't have to envision. It is impossible for us to forget.

But what about the third and fourth generation survivors? It is our obligation to make sure that they do not forget. They did not experience the devastation and destruction. It is for them what the Haggadah teaches us. They must envision as if they were there. They must envision as if they, together with their families, were taken and put in those boxcars. They must envision as if they were brought to the camps.

It is therefore our obligation to teach them, to tell them what life was like, whether we are a survivor or even a second generation survivor.

Tell them what it's like to live without having a bubby or a zeidy. Tell them what it's like not being able to sleep over at your cousin's house, because you have no cousins. Hitler did this to us. And not just to us, but to many Jewish families. He killed six million Jews, one and a half million Jewish children. They must know. For if they don't, we have lost our identity.

Stephen M. Goldman

There is no more impactful way to impart history than in the words of a witness. This is not just true in court, but is even more important for major historical events. This book, the story of one Holocaust survivor, Michael Weiss, is such a testimony.

There are historians who write and talk about the Holocaust, there are teachers who instruct their students about it, there are even those who deny the Holocaust in an effort to raise themselves above those who were there. However, Michael has, in this book, born witness to the evil that was the Holocaust and its perpetrators. He was there, the memories are seared into his very soul, and the words ring true.

Now, as the numbers of witnesses, survivors, World War II veterans, and exiles are sooner rather than later not going to be with us, it is our duty, our mandate and our responsibility to see to it that these stories are not forgotten. It is our moral imperative to tell our children, their children to one hundred twenty generations the truth, in order that mankind not repeat the errors of the past.

Thank you, Michael, for making your story available to all who will listen and heed the warnings of generations past. We, each of us, must become the witnesses for the witness, lest that this story be forgotten.

Elliott Weinhouse, M.D.

Can the world really forget the most infamous Holocaust in human history? Probably not. The world just pretends to forget so that anti-Semitism can flourish once again as it has for over two thousand years. Actually, anti-Semitism is becoming more apparent and blatant, especially in Europe (which is quite ironic).

The Europeans traded six million Jews for twenty million Islamic Arabs many who are nurturing and fostering this recent surge in anti-Semitism. Rational people cannot deny historical facts and evidence, but irrational people who are willing and even proud to sacrifice their children as suicide bombers easily pretend that there was no Holocaust. Furthermore, rabid anti-Semites in academic circles foster and kindle this Holocaust denial and just add fuel to this widespread evil denial.

Jewish people comprise a tiny, insignificant percentage of the world's population, but have contributed relatively more to science and medicine than any other ethnic group in history. Who can deny this proven, well-documented fact?

Instead of hating us, the world should shower us with appreciation. Six million innocent victims ... one and a half million innocent children ... we must never forget them.

───※───

Rabbi Ari Kostelitz

"And to them will I give in my house and within my walls a memorial and a name (a "yad vashem") ... that shall not be cut off." (Isaiah, 56:5)

It is memory that has helped us to last through thousands of years of history. Our religion and our people are founded on the collective memory of revelation at Har Sinai. Throughout the Torah we are commanded to remember: Remember the Shabbos day (Shmos 20:8), Observe the Shabbos as a reminder of the Creation (Shmos 20:11) and of the Exodus (Devarim 5:15); Remember, continually, the Exodus; Remember what the evil Amalek did. All those memories define us and help us keep focused on the goal of our national mission.

As the Baal Shem Tov (the founder of Chassidism) taught, "Forgetfulness leads to exile while remembrance is the secret of redemption."

There are few periods of time in history that are darker or more shocking than the Holocaust. And while the majority of people today understand at least vaguely what the Holocaust was, there are actually a growing number of younger people that don't fully understand or even know what it involved. Taking the time to understand the basics of the Holocaust is important.

We at our shul (Congregation Dovid Ben Nuchim) are extremely fortunate to have Mr. Michael Weiss as a congregant. Michael, a Holocaust survivor, has taken upon himself to share his testimony and teach, educate and speak about the Holocaust. He has spoken to countless audiences and gives tours at the local Holocaust museum here in Michigan. Not everyone has the opportunity to hear, in person, from a Holocaust survivor. We feel very privileged to have Michael share his story with us. At this time, Michael has written a book in which he has described all the horrors and experiences he went through.

Mr. Weiss has established a beautiful family here in Michigan and derives much *nachas* from his children, grandchildren and great grandchildren.

As Zvi Kopolovich, Holocaust survivor, wrote: "And so, within seven months, I lost my father, my brother, and my mother. I am the only one who survived. This is what the Germans did to us, and these are things that should never be forgotten. On the other hand, we had our revenge: the survivors were able to raise magnificent families – among them myself. This is the revenge and the consolation."

Michael Weiss personifies this with his lovely family .

Gary Torgow

One of the epic stains on the history of mankind, was the systematic and barbaric murder of six million of our brethren at the bloody hands of the Nazis in World War II. These atrocities were exacerbated by a deafening silence and a blinded eye by much of the rest of world civilization. Many of our planets citizens stood by as early as the 1930s, while Hitler and his henchmen began a public discrimination, humiliation and ultimately incarceration and murder of Jews throughout the European theatre.

The loss for the Jewish people was incomprehensible. In 1935, the population of European Jews was over nine million; by the end of World War II, two out of every three Jews had been annihilated by the Nazi killing machine. It was without a doubt, one of mankind's greatest failures and horrific losses.

As a Jew born into the post WWII era in America, my direct association with the Holocaust came through the *Shareis Haplayta*, the Holy survivors, who miraculously escaped the ashes of Europe. They are the treasures of our generation and have become for so many the picture of truth and undeniable faith in the complicated times we find ourselves.

One such giant, is our own Reb Meir Yehuda Ben Avrohom Yitchak, Mr. Michael Weiss, born in 1924 in Koson, Czechoslavakia. At the tender age of 17, Meir Yehuda and his family were forced into the Jewish ghetto and ultimately transported to Auschwitz, to Buchenwald and finally to Zeitz, where young Michael Weiss was liberated by the American Armed Forces.

His story, like so many, is one of miracles, and perseverance and incredible fortitude. His remarkable Emunah, and unshakable faith, are the foundational view that we, his beloved friends and neighbors witness each time we interact with Reb Meir Yehuda.

He has become for so many of us, the living embodiment of the Rambam-Maimonides, historic and critical Principles of faith, which serve as the underpinnings of our relationship with the Almighty.

Standing alongside Mr. Weiss as he daily pronounces the Kaddish or leads the Tehillim recitation in our shul, may seem to us a bit routine, but in reality, as each word or phrase is recited, it most assuredly is the cause of tremors and thunderbolts in the heavenly spheres above.

It is our collective hope and prayer that our dear and beloved friend, Mr. Michael Weiss will continue to inspire and encourage us and to illuminate the world around us until, 120.

May the words written in this book serve as both a constant reminder and a critical message of hope and perseverance!

Jim MacDonald

I had the wonderful privilege of taking Mr. Weiss' thoughts, words, experiences and emotions and placing them in print. Like many of you, my familiarity and knowledge of the Holocaust was limited, gained through a school textbook, occasional footage on a PBS television show or clips from a film/movie. I had a "youthful/minimal" understanding that an evil man (Adolf Hitler) did evil things to Jews with evil intentions.

I am thankful now as an adult I have the understanding I would be doing something significant, one of the more important things I'll ever do in my life, by being a part of sharing Mr. Weiss' story. This "first-person" view of Mr. Weiss' life before, during and after the Holocaust will give you, the reader, a direct connection to the host of emotions Mr. Weiss was feeling, as well as allowing you to clearly picture in your mind's eye each and every step of his journey! I thank Mr. Weiss for this opportunity, but more importantly, for his friendship.

I know for a fact, upon completion of this book, that you will feel educated and inspired. Get ready for a most revealing and intimate self-portrait!

With my friend, Jeno Roth.

From Kaszony To Auschwitz To Detroit

CHIMNEYS
– AND –
CHAMBERS

The Lingering Smell Of The Holocaust

Growing Up In Kaszony

I was born in 1924 in a little village in the Carpathian Mountains, which was called Kosino in Czech, and Kaszony (Mezokaszony) in Hungarian.

My father, Adolf Weisz, was born October 7, 1896, in Baranya (Boronya). My mother was Hermina (Herszkowicz) Weisz. My grandparents on my father's side were Lajos and Fanny (Gottfried) Weisz.

At the time of my birth, this area was located in the newly established country of Czechoslovakia in Eastern Europe. Czechoslovakia was established in 1918 right after World War I, and it was at this time that the new country assumed political control over the Carpathian Mountains. Czechoslovakia was a Republic with laws which protected its citizens.

Kaszony was a small, beautiful town deep in the Carpathian Mountains. On a clear night, the skies were full with beautiful, shiny stars. You could smell the fresh air. No factory smoke polluted the air.

We, the Jewish people, lived in peace with our neighbors. It was a time of prosperity, and we shared in this prosperity with everyone involved. Many Jews succeeded in living comfortably.

Our community where I was born was blessed over the generations with many people who lived their lives according to our ancient Jewish tradition. Not only the rabbi, but the shochet, the chazzan and other scholars exhibited their love of the Jewish people and Torah.

Also the merchants, the ordinary folks, the poor people, did not stray from the laws of the Torah. The very holiness that surrounded the Jews of our community added to their strength so that they were able to overcome the constant struggle, and later, the constant anti-Semitism, which was all

around us in Europe.

One could feel the holiness especially during holidays and special days on the Jewish calendar.

I recall starting kindergarten at the age of five. I woke up in the morning at 5 a.m. and arrived at "cheder," the Jewish school, at 6 a.m. until 8 a.m. We said our morning prayers and then we started learning Talmud. Then I went to public school until 4 p.m. I then came back to Hebrew School until 7 p.m. I kept this schedule five days a week. When I started kindergarten, I could only speak Yiddish. I grew up in a Jewish section of town.

Everyone in the community of Kaszony knew everyone else from their daily contacts. The marketplace and the surrounding business section was in the center of town. In

Rabbi Yisrael Tzvi Halevi Rottenberg

Rabbi Yisrael Tzvi Halevi Rottenberg, known as the Kaszonyer Rebbe, was born in 1890 and served his congregation from 1919 until his death in the Holocaust in 1944. His great grandfather was Rabbi Tzvi Hirsh from Bezidisow, Galicia, the author of Ateret Tzvi (The Crown of the Deer), and the student of the HaChozeh, the Seer of Lublin.

His father was Rabbi Yosef Halevi Rottenberg, who was probably the first Kaszonyer Rebbe. Rabbi Yosef was considered to be one of the fathers of Chassidus in the area and his yeshivah in Kaszony was well-respected. He died in 1911. After his death, his oldest son, Rabbi Chaim Shlomo Rottenberg became the rabbi of Kaszony. He died in 1919. After his death, the Jews of Kaszony picked Rabbi Yosef's youngest son, Yisrael Tzvi, to become their rabbi. He was considered one of the great scholars in Torah.

one courtyard, we had the main synagogue where most of our congregation worshiped. Right next to it was another place of worship which was called the "Bet HaMidrash." This is where our esteemed Rabbi Yisrael Tzvi Rottenberg prayed and learned with the students of the Yeshivah high school. There were 80 to 90 young men from ages 15 to 20 years old, who studied in the Yeshivah, or until they got married.

The students stayed at homes all over town which had a spare bedroom and the young men would pay a small fee to stay there. Most Yeshivahs at that time did not provide food for their students. The well-to-do ate at a Menzo (like a restaurant); they had three meals a day. Those who couldn't afford this, ate at Jewish homes, usually a different house each day. This system was called "essen teg." Most of these young people were from other towns. They came from all over the country. Just a few of us were from the same town.

Even the families who did not have very much, had at least a small garden in which vegetables such as tomatoes, cucumbers, green peppers, corn and green beans were grown. Many of us had some fruit trees in the backyard growing apples, pears, and peaches.

I remember my mother, Chana, God avenge her death, would wake up at 3 a.m. each Friday or on the eve of a holiday to bake the traditional challot (a special bread made for Shabbos). For the coming week, she baked bread. From then on, the cleaning and the traditional cooking went on for the entire afternoon.

No Jewish family in Kaszony considered themselves poor as long as they could manage to have Shabbos food, which included the challot, wine, fish, and meat or chicken.

Every Shabbos was very beautiful! Our house was clean as always!

In Kaszony, the Jewish people followed the Torah laws to eat kosher food. There were two slaughterhouses; one for cattle and one for poultry, and we had two butchers. They would go to the farmers and buy the cow, calf or lamb. The animals would be butchered on Thursday, ready for the Jewish families to prepare for Shabbos. When the holy days fell during the week, the shochet would prepare the animals earlier. Since we did not have refrigeration like today, the shochet's schedule for when meat would be ready was very important for his customers.

There was also Market Day every Monday. The ladies went out to the market and bought a chicken, goose or duck and brought it home. First the shochet would appropriately butcher the fowl according to Jewish law, and then it was brought back home for the next stage. The feathers would be plucked and then the fowl was washed, soaked and salted to complete the process of making it kosher and ready to cook. Typically chicken soup was made, what we Jews often call "Jewish Penicillin" because it seems to make a person feel better after having a bowl of it.

Another European tradition was to make a special stew-like dish called "cholent" for Shabbos. This was made from meat, beans and barley. Along with other dishes for the Shabbos lunch, like "kugel" and "kishke", the food would be taken by the children to the bakery on Friday afternoon. The baker would then put the food in the oven so that it could cook and stay warm until the children would pick it up on Shabbos morning. This procedure was followed to conform to the Torah laws for preparing food for Shabbos. We continue this tradition today. The cholent makes for a delicious lunch, especially in the winter.

Minutes before sunset, everyone in the family assembled at the Shabbos table, which was covered with a white tablecloth. We watched my Bubby (my grandmother Esther), she was over 100 years old, light the Shabbos candles (God bless her soul!). Then my mother Chana (God bless her soul) also lit her candles and said the blessing, welcoming Shabbos. They were the queens of our family!

After candle lighting, the men went to "shul" (synagogue) for the evening services. Mordechai Felberbaum, and his sons led the service, chanting our holy prayers. Their voices were beautiful. He was the shochet in Kaszony.

After the conclusion of the services, we hurried home to our Shabbos table. The entire family joined together and sang "Shalom Aleichem", the traditional melodious words welcoming the angels of peace into our home.

We sang the words from Proverbs, "Eshes Chayil", a hymn that recognizes both the women of the home, and Shabbos itself.

My Zeidy (my grandfather, God bless his soul) recited the

Rabbi Yisrael Tzvi Rottenberg (center) on a Shabbat walk.

Kiddish. This prayer is in recognition of God's creation of the world, and observing the seventh day (Shabbos) as a day of rest. This blessing is usually said holding a cup of wine, but many times during the winter we didn't have wine. When that happened, Zeidy would hold and bless the challot. The beautifully braided challot were placed on the table and covered with an ornate white cloth until it was time to say the "Hamotzi", the blessing on the challot.

On Shabbos morning, we returned to shul. The women prayed in the upper section of the synagogue, called the Ezrat nashim (women's section). After an inspiring holy service which lasted about three hours, we went home and had the second meal of our holy Shabbos and we sang Zemirot, the songs for the Shabbos. We finished the meal with "Bircat HaMazon," the prayers to our Holy God, thanking Him for our food.

My home was not a rich home. We did not have electricity or running water. If you wanted water, you had to go to the well and bring it in. We didn't have carpeting, it was a dirt floor. I can picture it now, it was one room. In the middle

31

Mezőkászony   *Utcarészlet*

Street view in Kaszony.

of the room we had our kitchen. To my right I lived with my parents. To my left is where my grandmother lived after my grandfather died.

My mother, God bless her soul, took care of my grandmother. She was a very old lady, as I remember her. When anyone asked how old she was, she said 100, year after year, because she did not remember how old she was!

When I was a child, I didn't have toys like children have today. We played with buttons, walnuts and simple things like this. At that time, there was a well for water in every yard. Our well was about fifty feet from my front door. I have memories of bringing to the house pails of water in the wintertime. It was very difficult to draw water because the wells were frozen. You had to break the ice before you could get a pail of water.

The streets in Kaszony were not paved at all. When the snow fell, we took, instead of a wagon, a sled and then attached the horse to the sled. This is how we got around! In the spring when the snow melted, we changed from the sled back to the wagons.

Yes, life in Kaszony was very hard in the winter. It was so cold you could walk on top of the snow. That is how hard and crisp the snow became! In the spring, it was very muddy from all the water that ran off from the snow in the mountains. There were no modern conveniences; no running water and no furnaces. Many times our neighbors supplied the Jews with wood and other products. However, almost each Jewish family had a cow or two to supply milk. Some had horses, but very few who made their living as wagoneers. Some Jews owned fields, and our friends, the gentiles, worked the land in return for a certain percentage of the crop. They were partners, like sharecroppers.

In those days, Jewish women in Kaszony didn't have much entertainment. They found ways to socialize in very original and productive ways. During the winter, Jewish women in Kaszony got together in the evening to help each other pluck feathers for bedding or peel corn from the cob. From those feathers they would make a down comforter and pillows. This was given to the girls when they got married as a wedding gift. During the social evenings, the women sang Yiddish and Hebrew songs. They told stories about their families and discussed events of the times.

On November 9, 1937, at the age of 13, I had my Bar Mitzvah. This brings back a lot of pleasant memories, but little did I know that a year later, an event on this date would change our lives.

I remember this Shabbos very well. I walked with my parents and grandparents to the synagogue. I used to get a new suit once a year for Passover, but for my Bar Mitzvah, I got

*1939 - The students in Yeshivat Ateret Tzvi in Kaszony.
I am in the top row (circled).*

a new suit with long pants. My mother, father, grandmother and grandfather also got new outfits. It was a very happy time for my family. My grandfather gave me a pocket watch which I proudly placed in my vest pocket. I remember that my rabbi and friends were in the shul, too. Following the services, there was a "kiddish." It was not like here in this country (the USA) so blessed by God, but I remember we had herring and cake and that my mother, God bless her soul, made cholent. I remember it was very delicious and I still have that taste in my mouth. Words of Torah learning, and blessings for the food were said.

This occasion of my Bar Mitzvah was and will always be one of my favorite memories.

Jewish settlers arrived in Hungary in the 1800s from Galicia and Poland. We Jews adopted the Hungarian language, but at home or with our friends, we spoke Yiddish, the Jewish language.

In my little village, about sixty percent owned small stores and workshops. These people usually owned their own homes. A large majority had only an eighth grade public school education. Most of them had marketable professions. These groups included the butchers, tailors, bakers, carpenters and painters. We also had a small group of storekeepers including clothing and shoe stores, grocers and yard goods and hardware stores. They were completely dependent on favorable business clients.

The population in Kaszony was around 2,500 people. We had about 90 Jewish families, 600 to 700 people.

About one-third of our population, a small group, consisted of big businessmen and the rich property owners. These were the more educated people. They were the teachers and the bankers. We also had those who also worked in public offices, the mayor. Our group also had doctors, lawyers and pharmacists. Then we had a few wealthy property owners including lumberyard and mill owners and those in possession of at least 100 acres of land. They hired workers, and grew wheat, corn, tobacco and grapes. Wine was made in large quantities. These goods were sent all over the country.

Many of the stores were Jewish-owned. They were all closed on Shabbos and Yuntuf (holy days). Almost every Jewish person attended the services in the synagogue on those days.

Preparing For Passover

For Passover (Pesach), we cleaned and painted our house. We changed the strawsack, which was a straw-filled sack made to fit our beds. (In those days, we did not have mattresses.) We changed the straw twice a year, at Passover and Rosh Hashana.

Food preparation for Passover began during the winter season, a few months before the holiday.

The ladies had the first job. On market day, which took place on Mondays, they shopped for nice and plump ducks, geese and chickens. These were brought home, and for the next few weeks these birds were fed very well until it was time to take them to the shochet.

Some people actually forced the animals to eat more than what they would have eaten naturally. This is called "shtopen" in Yiddish, to overly fatten them. This was not a practice in keeping with the Jewish law, which forbids causing any living creature to suffer. My mother did not follow this procedure of shtopen. She was a very kind person, and very observant. However, there were many families in Kaszony who had this custom.

When our geese and chickens were ready to be slaughtered, my mother took them down to the river with some of the other women in Kaszony. Since it was wintertime, the river was frozen. They had to break through the top layer of ice first in order to wash the feathers of the birds so they would be very clean. Like during the year, pillows and quilts were made from these feathers.

They took the clean birds to the shochet to be slaughtered. At home, my mother had to finish the process of kashering the meat. First she plucked the feathers (this was a big job!), and then opened the bird and took the insides out ("kishkes"). Then she soaked the raw meat for an hour and salted it for a half hour. It was then rinsed and ready to be cooked. My mother took the skins off and put them into a skillet and let them cook until they were brown. This is called greven. The fat, what we call shmaltz, was placed in a big jar for Pesach.

It was the tradition in Kaszony, as it was in many other towns in Carpathia, that the shochet would cut off one leg from the bird and put it aside. After he accumulated a number of these legs, he would give them to the poor people of Kaszony. This was done only during the Hebrew calendar months of Tevet and Shevat (the winter months). From the legs, they made tasty dish called "Pechah." This was fat. It could be made from the duck, goose or chicken. The fat was placed into a jar and we kept it for Pesach. As the winters in the Carpathian Mountains were very cold, there was no problem of spoilage.

We also enjoyed a variety of dishes made from potatoes – kugel, latkes, farfel – because potatoes were cheap!

The more observant families in Kaszony made arrangements to buy only wheat that had been "watched" from the moment it was cut in the field. Most important, this wheat had to stay dry so that it wouldn't accidentally start to rise or leaven. The matza baked from the special wheat is known as "Matza Shmurah" which means "guarded" matza. This special matza was eaten by the Rabbis and very religious people. There were families in Kaszony who bought "regular" wheat for Passover also.

Before Purim, the community began to prepare the wheat for grinding into flour for the matza. Neighbors would gather in one of their homes around a long, thin table covered with a tablecloth. There would be no question of even a single particle of chametz or leavened bread being hidden on its surface. Wheat would be spilled over the table with care. The neighbors would help pick through the kernels of the wheat, removing the impurities, stones, or bugs. Even a split kernel was cast aside. In this way, we ended up with the very best and clean wheat available to bake the matzas.

Baking the matza was a little business for someone, so first it had to be decided who would get the right to bake the matza. This was a decision which was put to a vote by the elders of the community. They gathered for that purpose at least two months before Passover in our shul.

In Kaszony, we had a number of people who bid for the right to bake the matza. The person would submit, in a sealed envelope, the price that he would sell the matzas to the community. Because so many of the Kaszony Jews were very poor, the price had to be affordable, since eating the matza was a religious requirement. The matza symbolizes the bread of affliction and the journey from Egypt.

The sealed envelope was opened by the president of the community. I still remember him, Lajos Ackerman. He was a sergeant in the Army during the First World War and he wore many decorations on his uniform. His daughter lives in New York, and the way I remember ... he had two sons whom I haven't had the chance to meet yet here in America. That year, 1944, the lowest bid had been submitted by Herschel Kuferstein. In addition to the low price, he was a man who had other good qualities and points in his favor. He was a "melamed" a teacher of one of the better "chadarim" (Hebrew school). He also was a religious man, a "Yareh Shamayim", who feared our God in Heaven.

We had one mill in town. Early one morning, a small group of Kaszony Jews sat in a horse and wagon to go to kosher the mill, meaning to make the mill fit for Passover use. Mr. Johnesen Weisz, and the "shamash" (sexton), checked again the millstone. After they were satisfied, the process of koshering began. Everything that was a part of the milling process was completely cleaned and scrubbed. The Rabbi of our community, Yisrael Tzvi Rottenberg, was called to give the final inspection of the premise. Once he gave his approval that everything was according to the Jewish code of law, the grinding to make the Passover flour started.

The first wheat to be ground was the guarded wheat for the "Matza Shmurah." The reason for this was that if the regular wheat had been ground first, any leftover grains would mix with the guarded wheat and that would bring down the guarded wheat to the level of the regular wheat.

Four weeks before Passover we started to bake the matzas. There were quite a few of us teenagers who worked in the matza factory.

There are some very important and serious Jewish laws that have to be followed in order to bake a kosher matza for Passover. We started out putting the matza flour into a dish and then adding water to it. There was a man whose job was to knead the dough. The flour placed into the dish had to be the same weight each time. The water was then added to it. After this, no more flour could be added. From the time the water touched the flour, that particular batch had to be finished and baked in 18 minutes for it to be a kosher matza.

This was the last time matzas were baked in my hometown and the surrounding communities.

A few days before Pesach, I took the Pesach dishes down from the attic for my mother. This is where we stored everything during the year that we used for the week-long holiday.

The dishes were covered and put on special shelves so that no "chametz" (anything leavened) would come in contact with them.

We made borscht from red beets in a small barrel which was one of our main dishes during the eight days of Passover. Details of how it was made I do not know. The only thing I remember is that my mother, God bless her soul, cut the beets into pieces, and with salt, put them into the small barrel. Somehow this developed into such a fine dish. We ate them with potatoes. I still have the taste in my mouth.

The Beginning Of The Holocaust

November 9-10, 1938, became a 48-hour period that we Jews cannot ever forget. We call it Kristallnacht. (Crystal Night or The Night of the Broken Glass). The German police and the soldiers conducted a pogrom that was organized by the Nazi government against the Jewish people. The Nazis murdered and imprisoned thousands of Jewish people in concentration camps. The Nazis burned our synagogues and thousands of our holy Torah scrolls. Gravestones in the Jewish cemeteries were overturned and destroyed.

The Germans used the event of a 17-year-old boy, Herschel Gryznspan, who killed a German official in Paris in a reaction to

Diplomat Shot; Nazis Aroused

Jews Face Reprisals for Paris Attack

BERLIN, Nov. 7—(A. P.)—The official correspondence service Dienst aus Deutschland charged that "international Jewry" was responsible for the attempt of a Polish Jewish refugee from Germany to assassinate the secretary of the German Embassy in Paris today.

The service indicated that Jews in Germany probably would have to pay for the attempt on Ernst von Rath, the embassy secretary, by an assailant who gave his name as Herschel Gryznspan, 17 years old, formerly of Hanover, Germany.

Anti-Jewish feeling here was aggravated by the incident, which was displayed on the front pages of all newspapers under flaring headlines.

Germany's treatment of his parents and thousands of other Polish Jews, as the pretense for Kristallnacht.

Here are two eyewitness reports of what happened in two cities in Germany on Kristallnacht.

Herschel Gryznspan.

"Shortly after 6 o'clock in the morning of November 10, 1938, the synagogue was torched, and its furnishings and ceremonial objects destroyed in the fire. The interior of the adjoining school building was also destroyed. The fire brigade stood by to prevent damage to the neighboring buildings. What remained of the walls of the synagogue was completely torn down before the end of the War." [1]

"I was 15 years old, and on my way home from school. There was commotion in the street. People were pointing to smoke which seemed to poison the air. Being curious, I followed the smoke. The smoke billowed from the burning of my beloved synagogue. The fire had already consumed the biggest part of the building." [2]

In the period of the Holocaust years, Jews lived in a society where they were hated and every effort was made to destroy their values.

The Holocaust was a well-organized and a well-prepared plan by the German government, utilizing modern techniques. Under the code name, "Final Solution," the Nazis developed a plan to annihilate the Jewish people. It was Hitler's creation. It was, in simple terms, a plan to kill every Jew in Europe in the lands they conquered, and probably at some point, the

---

1   Gottlieb, Fred; "My Childhood In Siegburg"; Mazo Publishers, 2008; 56. In October 1985, the Siegburg municipality erected a memorial fountain at the site of where the synagogue once stood. Written on the plaque: At this site stood, since 1841, the synagogue of the Jewish community, comprising more than 300 members. On November 10, 1938 the synagogue fell victim to the flames of the Pogrom Night ("Reichkristallnacht"). Under the Nazi tyranny, the majority of the community's members were murdered. Let their death be a warning to us.
2   Ringer Nenner, Brigitte; Brigitte's Angel Of Poetry: Eyewitness To Kristallnacht and The Concentration Camps; Mazo Publishers, 2014.

Jews in the rest of the world.

Hitler created new jobs for the Germans, perfecting the way to kill ... How to remove resistance from the masses ... How to efficiently move millions of humans ... How to select slaves ... How to terrorize ... How to process the dead.

And to the surprise of the Jews, Hitler's plan was receptive to the Germans and other Europeans. Thus the Holocaust.

Estimated Number Of Jews Murdered In The "Final Solution"

In 1938, Czechoslovakia, which bordered with Hungary, was overrun by the Germans, and the Hungarian government took control. As a token of appreciation, Hitler gave part of the Carpathian Mountains to Hungary. This included my small village of Kaszony. We Jews of Kaszony were destined to come under the rule of the Hungarian fascist government under the Hungarian fascist army. Right then and there, it was the end of a happy youth in a quiet, peaceful and small town where my family lived for many generations.

I remember in the morning when the Hungarian Army crossed the border into Czechoslovakia, we Jews went out with the rest of the population to greet them. We put our Hungarian flags up, and there were many older Jewish men who put on their uniforms who fought in World War I in the Austro-Hungarian Army. Many were officers well-decorated with medals on their uniforms. (Both of my grandfathers served in the Austro-Hungarian armies.) The Jewish war veterans tried to assure us it would be all right for the Jews under Hungarian government. But then there were people like my parents, who discussed this, and were afraid.

We knew already that Hitler did not like Jews. Soon after the Hungarian conquest, they decreed harsh ordinances against the Jews. The first victim to fall was Josel Braunstein, who was shot on the first evening of occupation while on his way home after the evening service at the shul. That first victim was an indication of what the Jews of Kaszony and of the entire country could expect. The Hungarian government, under the reign of Admiral Horthy, instituted racial laws against the Jews of Hungary – which included the Jews of Kaszony.

These anti-Jewish laws were already enforced throughout Nazi-occupied Europe. In a couple of weeks, laws started to come out of Budapest. Anti-Semitic laws, racist laws and all these laws were aimed at us Jews.

Every Jew was required to wear a yellow star, a Jewish

A woman selling arm bands with the Star of David.

Star of David on their outer clothing. Jews were forbidden to conduct business, they were forbidden to practice their profession. Their radios were confiscated and they were forbidden to leave their homes in the evening.

The Jewish Star of David was almost like a code word that wherever a Jew would go, it would be known that they were Jewish. This indicated that a person was not protected by the local, federal or state governments.

It happened many times that people went to local Jewish businesses and bought merchandise, but never paid for it, and there was no law to protect the Jewish merchant.

There was another law which said that Jews could not go to college. I was an only child to my parents. I remember my parents were saving up money for my education. The money was never used for my education and I never went to college, because I'm a Jew.

Then another law came out. Any Jewish professional who had a license had it taken away. In my family, there was only one cousin who finished college. He finished medical school but never got his license. He never practiced as a doctor. He was sent to Auschwitz and never came home.

The Jews were ordered to register at the town hall and present documents to prove their citizenship. The leadership of Kaszony of the Jewish community was ordered to present to the authorities names of all Jews who lived in Kaszony. They used this information for the deportations to Ukraine, for the draft of males into forced labor units for all kinds of work that the Kaszonyer Jews had to perform for the town. Jewish teenagers were forced to serve in the "Levente" (youth battalions).

Then it came, the first wave of deportation from Kaszony to the town to Kamenets-Podolsk in Ukraine. Some Jews who lived in Kaszony for many generations were deported because they didn't have all of the documents needed. The Hungarian soldiers marched our fellow Jews, men, women, children and the elderly across the border. During the day, they were marched further and further ... during the nights they concentrated them in large barns and other structures.

The Hungarian government knew very well what was in store for the Jews in the Ukraine wilderness. The Hungarian support units that Ukraine volunteered and the German Einsatzgruppin (SS killing units) perpetrated a terrible slaughter of the Carpathian Jews, which among them were about one hundred Jews from Kaszony. The murderers lined up the Jewish families, in Kamenets-Podolsk in Ukraine and machine-gunned them with brutality.

The second great blow fell upon the Jews of Kaszony when the Hungarians mobilized all Jewish males, ages 18-50 into Munko Tabor (forced labor units). Hundreds of men ... fathers ... sons ... brothers ... cousins ... brothers-in-law were taken into forced labor and organized into army-like units under the command of the Hungarian army. Many of these units were sent to the front lines in Ukraine, Russia, Germany, Italy and Hungary. They were digging their tunnels, trenches and rail lines. Fortifications were also built like bunkers.

In one of those units was my father. He was sent to the Russian front. His job was to pick up the dead and wounded. It was a very dangerous job. He was there for two years. When he came home, his fingers and toes were frozen. He was not the same man I knew ... He was a tailor, and after this experience he couldn't work in his profession any longer.

Tens of thousands of Jews in those forced labor units died from hard labor, starvation, sickness, frostbite, and enemy actions at the hands of fanatically anti-Semites. Many sons from Kaszony were shot or simply perished. Some of the units that remained in Hungary performed similar work. They too suffered from the brutality of Hungarian officers and many times were in deadly danger. My father told us that near his barrack there was a big gym where there were thousands of people in forced labor. There was a rumor going around that in that barrack people were sick with typhus. The Germans locked the doors with barbed wires and they set the gym on fire. Those who broke out of the sides of the gym to escape were machine-gunned by the German soldiers. When my father tried to talk about it, he ended up crying to the point of hysterics and got sick.

Ultimately, the final expulsion of the remaining Kaszonyer Jews left Kaszony "Judenrein", meaning "empty of Jews" as was the rest of the country.

There is a well-known Jewish proverb which says the apple doesn't fall far from the tree. But when there is a storm, the apple could be carried away very, very far. Hitler's brutal storm carried and scattered us from our little town of Kaszony to all corners of the globe. When I think or mention this word "Kaszony," it's like I would touch a very soft, delicate spot. It hurts. It hurts very much. In that word, there is hidden a fountain of remembrance.

That place, that little town of Kaszony is surrounded by so much love. Our parents, grandparents, brothers and sisters, friends, neighbors and landsman were the foundation for this love. We had an identity ... we were somebody. There was pure and unpolluted love. All our feelings and actions were natural, nothing artificial. There were no evil deeds. No evil thoughts entered our minds.

In my home, we spent so much time in preparation for Shabbos and the holidays. This is how we lived our lives until the "storm" blew in, when the Hungarian government crossed the border into Czechoslovakia. The brutal, barbaric hurricane turned our lives upside down. Suddenly we became cattle-wagon passengers! We lost our dearest belief in humanity. We lost our identity.

During the years, many times I awaken and feel a rush of emotions. Sometimes it grabs me in the middle of a "simcha" (a joyous family occasion) like a seizure. I start to think, "How can I forget what happened to us? ... How can I enjoy myself? ... Am I allowed to take part in enjoyment after such a major tragedy happened to my family and my people?" Or if I am aggravated about something minor, I think to myself, "How can I let this bother me when my parents ... my family ... six million of my people ... perished in such a dreadful way?"

There are many nights when I cannot fall asleep, and tears begin to flow. My pillow is my only witness. I think of my small, loving town of Kaszony. My family, I love them all and I always think of them. I think of the six million martyrs who were killed so brutally in gas chambers and crematoriums, vanishing through the chimneys without so much as a grave. They are close to my heart.

It is our sacred duty to remind all those who don't know, who don't want to know and who don't want to be disturbed by such memories. To all those who are trying to deny our tragedy, we the witnesses, we are here to tell, to remember, the tragic truth in full!

Deportation To The Ghetto

In the Spring, the Jewish people observe the Passover holiday for eight days. We remember how Pharaoh, the King of Egypt, enslaved the Jews for hundreds of years, implementing the beginnings of forced work details.

In 1944, on the eighth day of Passover, a law came from Budapest (the Hungarian government), what was on a Saturday, that tomorrow (a Sunday), each Jew (the young, the old, the sick) had to leave their homes and go to the schoolyard. The law was written in the form of a poster which was posted all over town. Two of these paper signs were placed on our synagogue's door. We finished our holiday prayers with crying, with tears in our eyes because we had to go home and pack. We had to leave our own homes.

My grandmother was very old, as I remember her. She couldn't see. For me it is very hard to say "blind." If they would have let her stay in her home for a few weeks, or a few months at the most, she would have died in her bed, but we had to take her out of her sick bed. As a matter of fact, it was from her deathbed. And we had to take her with us to the schoolyard. I'm sure there were many elderly people just like her who had to go to the schoolyard.

There was a tall man with a shaved head seated by a table in the schoolyard. He had a list with everyone's name on it. He was a Presbyterian Minister. If someone was missing, he was very strict. We had to prove where the missing person was.

We slept there overnight (there was not one bed in the entire building). In the morning, they brought in horses and wagons and packed us on them. (The horses and wagons were all Jewish-owned). They took us to a big city which was called Beregszasz. We were ordered into a big brick factory. (If you could picture this with me ... we left two days ago from our home, with our children, with our families. In those two days, we had no access to hot water, so neither the children nor the adults could bathe. Everyone was filthy from this ordeal.

The weather in Europe at the time of Passover (the end of March) is still quite cold. The whole day it was drizzling. We went into the dark, long and empty barracks. The floor was mud and there were only a few poles holding up the roof. About 60 families were placed in the barracks. The ladies tied up sheets to the poles so they could have some privacy. The first thing each family did was search the ghetto for anything useful. We were able to bring bricks and make a kind of wall around the sides of the barrack to protect us from the elements. We spread our beddings on the floor before going to sleep. We slept close together because there wasn't very much room allotted to a family.

In the Beregszasz ghetto, the Kaszony Jews made efforts to organize themselves and adjust to this new situation. Prayer services were held three times a day inside the barracks and conducted by our Rabbi, Yisrael Tzvi Rottenberg.

Each family was responsible for their own meals. We tried to preserve as much as possible of the food we brought with us ... not knowing how long this would last. Outside the barracks in the field, we put together a few stones and bricks and made a makeshift cooking place. We gathered branches and pieces of wood to make a fire for cooking. Each lady tried to improvise and show her expertise in cooking.

Once a day, the ghetto management provided soup, but many of us didn't eat it since there was a question whether it was kosher. Only the small portion of bread that they gave us was eaten.

I remember that my mother, God bless her soul, tried to make all kinds of cookies from the matza pieces we brought with us from home, which lasted for a few weeks. Some farmers brought milk, bread and cheese to sell, but we didn't have any money. There were ladies who traded their wedding rings and other jewelry for the milk and bread for their families.

The men were ordered to shave their beards and peyot. Only Rabbi Yisrael Tzvi Rottenberg did not shave his beard and his helper Nutu Weisz wrapped his beard in a handkerchief to hide it from the enemy. Thinking about this, I don't really know how this was accomplished!

Some people tried to hide from the police. In our town grapes were grown, and some people had the idea that they would hide in the shack where the farming equipment was stored. Unfortunately, they were discovered after a few days. They surrendered to the police and they were shipped to the ghetto of Beregszasz.

Also there were a few women who were ready to give birth. They remained a short while in Kaszony, but even they were finally brought into the ghetto.

It seems that from all of the surrounding villages, there were common stories about Jews who tried to hide the fact that they were Jewish, but were eventually discovered and sent to the ghetto.

There was a man from Kaszony that we did not even know was Jewish, but the Nazis found out that he was hiding his real identity as a Jew, so he was brought to the ghetto. He never came to shul and did not have any religious contact with the Jewish community.

There were Jewish women who married non-Jews, but for some, being married to a Gentile did not help. We saw one woman who could not escape the Hungarian police being escorted to the ghetto. We, the Jews of Kaszony, could hardly believe it. We later heard the story that she told some of the Kaszony women her husband did not try to protect her, and was glad she was taken away. He told them that he was tired of being around Jews.

A memorial plaque to remember the Jews who died in Beregszasz in 1944.

There was a lady from Kaszony who acted like she lost her mind. She was running around in the ghetto yelling, "Save yourselves! Escape! Leave this place!" Some people thought maybe she wasn't crazy after all. Perhaps she saw what was going to happen.

A number of very sick people were taken from the ghetto to the town's hospital. Just a day before the deportation from Beregszasz to Auschwitz, all the sick were returned to the ghetto.

Poor hygienic conditions in the ghetto were a very big problem. There were more than 18,000 people concentrated in this small area. There were no shower facilities and no sewers.

We went to great lengths to keep clean. In order for someone to bathe, we had to bring water from the well and then heat up the water on a fire outside. From there, we brought in the water to the barracks in buckets.

The people who were in charge of the ghetto sent some of us to Beregszasz to work. I was sent to the synagogue. My job was to sort and organize piles of clothes that were taken from the Jews. The main benefit for me was that during this period of six weeks while I was in this ghetto was that I had a chance to buy food and other items we needed in the black market.

One morning, a Nazi came into the barrack and told us,

"Throw your money and jewelry into this bucket. If you do not do this, I will shoot you myself!"

As he went by, our rabbi showed him a watch not worth anything and said that he needed it for religious reasons (when to start the morning and evening prayers) and the Nazi said, "You can keep it." Then, another German officer came in a half-hour later and said, "If I find anyone hiding or not putting the valuables into the bucket, I will shoot you." He then went through the barrack and saw the watch of the rabbi. This officer jumped on the rabbi, holding the watch saying, "What is this?!" The rabbi explained again that he wasn't trying to hide it, and that the other officer said he could keep it. This officer didn't want to hear what the rabbi had to say, and he ordered the rabbi to go out to the yard. Then he ordered all of the people to come out into the yard and he told them, "This is what we do with people who don't obey our orders. The next person I find, I will get all of you out here and you will watch how I will shoot him myself." That German soldier had a whip with him always and he picked up his hands to crack the whip on the rabbi. I was sure that God wouldn't let this beast hit the rabbi. The rabbi, who believed in God's laws, the laws of Moses, this holy man, was hit on the head and bled profusely. How could this happen? I cannot describe my emotions. This entire incident made me very upset.

One of my friends buried his valuables outside the barracks. He said that if the German soldiers found the treasure, they would not know who it belonged to, and could not punish him. Later, he took those valuables to buy food and other necessities.

The valuables which the Hungarians and Germans confiscated from the Jews in the ghetto were kept until the war was over in the basement treasury of the Hungarian National Bank. Some say that with the valuables that the Hungarians robbed from the Jews, they paid the war reparations which were levied against them by the Allies. And there is a good portion of the valuables which serve now as the Hungarian Gold Reserve.

We learned quickly that everyone could not be trusted. There was a young man who was a sergeant in the Hungarian Army. He had a good friend in the ghetto, whose name was Gabi Weisz. He told him that he could escape. First he had to go to a hotel in the city, and then he would take him to Budapest and hide him there. Gabi Weisz escaped to the hotel, but his "friend" was there with the police. He was arrested and taken back to our ghetto. As far as I know, he never came home; I am sure he was killed in the gas chamber.

We, the Jews of Kaszony, and the rest of the Jews of our ghetto in Beregszasz didn't read the "writing on the wall" well enough. We never thought what would happen in the next month. We Jews did everything in order to delay our end ... except uprising and rebellion. I myself, I'm over 90 years old as I write this story. I've never held a gun in my hand; I wouldn't know how to shoot it. We weren't equipped or taught to kill people. When somebody said that we might all get killed or that we should escape, he was shouted down and told that he was spreading fear and despair, that in fact, it was his own fear.

At the beginning of the Hebrew month of Sivan, 5704 (1944), on the eve of the holiday of Shavuot, a rumor was spreading throughout the ghetto that all 18,000 Jewish people in the ghetto would be moved to a more secure place because the Soviet Army was advancing, and it was very close to Beregszasz.

However, there were others who maybe knew the fate of the Jews had been tragically decided. The Hungarian government brought in boxcars, and when I say brought in, I mean to the door of the barracks because the railroad tracks were already laid down. These cars used to pick up bricks but now they were picking up human beings, innocent

Jews from the Beregszasz Ghetto being forced into the boxcar.

Jewish people. They packed us in like sardines ... on the train to Auschwitz. It was very hot during the day and very cold at night. People were very thirsty. There were infants, children, parents and grandparents without anything to drink.

Eighteen thousand Jews meant eighteen thousand individuals. Just like people sitting next to you at home. I still can hear the whistle from the train. I remember one of my friends had a bottle of shnaps (whiskey). He gave everyone a little sip to make a "Lechaim", a toast to our health. Little did we know...

Many were sick, had a cold or fever from the ghetto. The children were crying because they were hungry and thirsty. The mothers were crying because their children were suffering. After everything we had gone through, our "Bitachon" (our belief) was still very strong.

When we asked a Hungarian soldier about where we were being taken, he said that we were going to be working and the children would have their own nursery.

We were able to talk with some of the Polish Jews who were in the camp. They told us that every young mother with a child should give the child to the grandmother or another older person.

The bulk of the transport from Hungary reached Auschwitz through Czechoslovakia with the freight trains. Each freight train was supposed to carry 45 people, but actually, they packed 80-100 people in each car, under unbearable conditions. Thousands of sick and elderly people as well as babies died on the train during the three-day travel from Beregszasz to Auschwitz due to no water, no food and no ventilation.

Now I would like to summarize: We were away from home for six weeks. We didn't have meals, hot or cold We had not had a shower. We didn't change our clothes. If you can ... look into the faces of those babies and children. Imagine how their mothers, fathers, their grandparents felt. They were sleepy, hungry, dirty. Their eyes cried out. They were depressed ... what they went through up until now ... it was inhumane.

What human being would take so many innocent people and kill them? How could the free world not see or smell the mass-murder and destruction of six million innocent human beings. How could they pretend not to hear, not want to know, to stop the genocide. How could such a terrible thing happen in the 20th century?

The Israeli poet Avraham Shlonsky, sums it up for us in his well-known poem, "An Oath to Remember".

"In the presence of eyes which witness the slaughter, which saw the oppression the heart could not bear, we have taken an oath, to remember it all. To remember, not once forget. Forget not one thing to the last generation."

Auschwitz

We were scared. What was going to happen to us? "Does anybody know where we are?" "Does anybody care about us?" One thing that we made sure to do, and we were happy about it, was to keep our families and relatives together.

The train stopped ... we got out of the boxcar ... We didn't know what was going to happen to us in this place. We came in front of a big gate and on the top it was written "Arbeit Macht Frei" which means "Work will make you Free." We were crossing into "hell" through the gate of Auschwitz.

As we stepped through the gate we heard screaming, babies crying, everybody crying and we heard the Germans only using one word "schneil" which means fast.

The Germans had these vicious dogs and they were jumping on everyone, women and children included.

Two selections were made; one was made as we came in.

They sent men to the right and women to the left. At this point, the Nazis divided the families. They did not care about people staying together. Try to visualize with me how this was. You could see and feel the devastation fathers, mothers and children had at that time. No one knew what was happening. Everyone was scared.

Then there was another selection. The soldiers would look at you ... and in that way they decided who would live and who would die. The "too young" (What is too young?! Too young was meant from infants to 15.) they sent to the right. The "too old" (What is too old?! Ages 40 and older?!) would also go to the right. I was sent to the left.

I remember coming in front of a big, long shiny building and by the door we were told "whatever you have in your hands, put on the ground, undress." We were shaved, got a shower, came out of the other side of the building. The sun was shining and it was May. We were handed a pair of pants, a shirt, a beret, and a pair of shoes. They did not care about the sizes so we exchanged the clothes among us to try to get something that would fit.

All of a sudden, somebody called my name. I asked myself, "Who knows me here? Who would call my name?" When I figured out who was calling me, I went to him and asked, "Who are you?" He told me his name. I knew this man my entire life. His name was David Klein! The only difference was that from the ghetto to Auschwitz, there were four different transports. He came with the first one and I came with the fourth one. Three weeks difference and the man wasn't recognizable due to the treatment he received during the time. When I knew him at home, he was a businessman, a gentleman with a full beard, always wearing a suit and tie.

As we were walking, the wind was blowing and I asked him, "I smell something very bad, what is it?" He started to cry and pointed with his finger to the chimneys. And then he said, "You see that building there ... that is a gas chamber." He saw I didn't understand so he explained it to me.

"All those people you came with an hour ago and were sent to the right, the ones they thought were too young, the ones they thought were too old, they could be in that building, in the gas chamber. The Nazis told those people that they were going to take a shower. Instead of water coming through the water pipes, poison gas comes through."

Since the time that we entered the concentration camp, and went through selections, I had not seen my mother or my father.

Our barracks in Auschwitz had bunk beds, four prisoners to a bed, and they handed the four of us one blanket.

Then the boxcars were brought back and they packed us in there. The only difference was when I was packed into the boxcar at the brick factory in Beregszasz, I had my parents with me, some of my Yeshivah friends, my rabbi, and other members of my family.

At this point, I didn't know anyone in the boxcar. They took us to Buchenwald. Buchenwald was a concentration camp with around 50,000 people of all nationalities. There were Germans, Poles, Hungarians, Romanians and others. Understand that in those days, in Germany, if somebody was suspected to be a Communist, or didn't follow Hitler's law exactly, they didn't need a judge or jury. They just took them to a concentration camp ... and I was told the majority were taken to Buchenwald.

Buchenwald was like a "grand central station" so to speak. If anybody needed help in Germany, as a matter of fact by then, all of Europe was Germany, they called up Buchenwald, and they sent them free labor. For example, when my wife was 14 years old, at that time I didn't know her, she was sent to an airplane factory with her sister Edith.

I stayed in Auschwitz for two weeks.

Buchenwald

We were transported to Buchenwald by boxcar. Again, we were stuffed into this awful transport. As I was looking around, I was almost in shock. At first, I didn't recognize who was right there near me ... I took a second look, and it was my father! But I couldn't yell, "How are you father?!" I couldn't move either and go to him. I was thankful to God!

After we were in Buchenwald, when I was able to get close to my father, naturally we talked about what happened to my mother. And we were crying and I tell you, between us, I don't think my father ever hugged me. But this day he hugged me and told me that he loved me.

We talked about when he was a young man and how he met my mother and how they lived. It was a hard life, but they were happy, especially when I was born, their only son. We also discussed his young life. It was also hard. His father didn't come back from the first World War.

I really got to know my father in those days in Buchenwald. After that, we couldn't talk much.

In the Torah, there is the story of our patriarch, Jacob, before he died. He called all his sons together and he spoke to them and he blessed them. And now, looking back on this time with my father, I believe that is what he was doing with me, between Auschwitz and Buchenwald, almost like he was saying goodbye to me.

We were in Buchenwald for about a week. The conditions were about the same as in Auschwitz. We got very little food.

They sent us out to work a few times on a truck. We had to clean up debris, most likely from bombings. The work itself was not hard, especially since I was young and I was together with my father.

I remember going through a yard where there were pigs.

The farmers gave them things to eat like potato peels, so when we went through there, everybody took what was still edible and just ate it, not thinking about the pigs and the mud. We were that hungry.

My father tried to keep a happy face. He told me, "Wir welen leben ... we are going to live through this" and he told me many times, "Der oybershter vil helfen ... God will help us. He always helped us, and He will help us this time."

Our sleeping place in Buchenwald.

My Personal Card in Buchenwald.

My Father's Personal Card in Buchenwald.

Zeitz

After about a week in Buchenwald, I, along with 4,000 others, was sent to a city called Zeitz. Zeitz is a small town near Leipzig in Germany. Our job was to build a factory which would make gasoline out of coal. Germany has a lot of coal, but no oil. We built that factory four times and it was bombed four times. We saw the bombs falling. We even saw the American stars on the planes. At the first bombing, none of our people got hurt, but during the second, third and fourth bombing, our people were wounded and killed. During the second bombing, my good friend with whom I started out in kindergarten was killed. His name was Tibi Schwartz. After liberation, I found his sister and told her that her brother was killed during the second bombing in the city of Zeitz.

When we arrived at Zeitz, we were placed in one barrack. The commander of the camp made a speech. He said, "You are in a concentration camp here, remember it forever. This is not a recuperation center. This is a concentration camp. Here you have to work – Arbeit Macht Frei. Work will make you a free person. If you do not work, you will be taken straight to the furnace ... to the crematorium. The choice is yours."

Our typical routine day in the camp was as follows: We were awakened at 5 a.m. The guards went through the barracks; in one hand they had a whistle, in the other hand a whip. The whistle and the whip were used. In minutes, all of us were out of the bunk-beds. There were no mattresses or pillows. We had to run to the latrine, and the washroom, all of us, at once. The latrine was a long barrack that served as a public outhouse. On one side was a row of faucets with cold water for washing.

As I mentioned, we were building a factory where we were

supposed to make gasoline out of coal. We had to grind the coal, and in order to wash off the coal dust our face and hands, we had to have soap, otherwise it was impossible in cold water to get clean.

A half-hour later, we had the morning roll call. We lined up in front of our barracks, five people across. We were told the tall people had to stand in the back row and the shorter people had to stand in rows in front of them. This way it made it easy for the Germans to see each face.

To stand in these lineups every morning and night, was a torture for us. Not only did we have to stand in the rain, cold, snow and wind, but it also served as a cruel form of punishment. The block commander, usually a German criminal, was also a prisoner. And the Kapos were mostly non-Jews. I had a couple of Kapos from Hungary. They really enjoyed beating me.

They counted and recounted the prisoners to make sure that all of us were present. But standing in those lines morning and evening, we prayed and cried to "Hashem" (to our God) every morning and evening while we were counted. We then marched from the camp to the factory, going through the city of Zeitz. We heard church bells ringing. It looked like they were religious people who went to church. I wondered what they prayed for because I do not think people who would go to church and pray would treat people in the manner in which we were treated. Like we were animals ... or worse!

One evening, we returned to the barrack after daytime work. We stood in line to be counted. I heard somebody saying "Tonight is Kol Nidrei." It was the holiest night of the year, meaning that it was Yom Kippur, which is a fast day. Then, we stood in line, waiting for our piece of bread with a spoon of jam and a piece of margarine. But we could not eat, because it was a fast day. Somehow, we fell asleep and we were awakened by the sound of the siren. It was an air raid!

In the morning, we were taken to a location to work at the

other end of the factory. We saw a big building underground, like a basement and on top of the roof there were three big holes. They took us down in that basement and we saw a lot of machinery on one side and ground up coal on the other side. From that coal, we were supposed to make gasoline. Then they gave us a bucket with a rope, and a person would go to the top of the roof by the hole. The people up there would tie the rope to the bucket and lower the bucket into the basement. We filled up the bucket with the coal and they pulled it up. The German soldiers didn't come down into the basement. We prayed and cried the entire day of Yom Kippur. Then we saw something shiny. Someone figured out it was a bomb that had not yet exploded! Thank God it didn't explode while we were there! We were told to come up and after that, we never went back there.

Sometimes my father and I were assigned to the same work detail. I didn't like this very much because I saw how hard they made my father work. Many times during our working day my father was beaten and kicked. I am sure he did not like it much either to see me being worked as hard as I was.

Before these events, my father typically enjoyed smoking a pipe at home. While we were working, we usually got five cigarettes a week. For myself, I would trade my cigarettes for a piece of bread. But my father wanted to smoke.

We were not allowed to talk with anyone in the work detail. But one night, when we were coming back to the barracks from the work detail, my father was telling me he wasn't sure how long he could continue to work like he was doing now ... and that I should always take care of my mother. Right there, an SS soldier saw us talking. He pulled both of us out of the line and told my father to slap my face. My father did not want to do this. The SS soldier then sent me back into the line with the rest of the people. A few minutes later, I saw my father running and he was being chased by this SS soldier. When he reached our line where I was, he could hardly see or talk ... he was bleeding from his nose and mouth. I almost fainted. We finally got to the camp and he washed up. I had two cigarettes saved, which I gave to him. He smoked one after the other. He smiled and really appreciated it!

Once a month, German officers came to our camp. I am not sure if they were really doctors, but they acted like they were and examined us. They looked at my father and told him that they would send him to a hospital. I was very happy because I thought he would sleep in a bed, he could relax a little, receive a decent meal. As a matter of fact, I told them I would like to go too, but they wouldn't let me. This was in October of 1944. In early 1945, these same doctors sent me to Buchenwald. I found out there is no such thing as sending a Jew to a hospital. All of those people they told they were sending to a hospital ... they were sent to a gas chamber instead. I have an official paper from the archives of Buchenwald which states exactly what happened to my father.

As the American army began to get closer to Buchenwald, the Germans were the only ones in our camp who knew this information. One indicator was that they closed the crematorium. At that point, when someone died, the only thing that could be done with the body was to place it near the barracks outside.

Liberation

There is saying, "everything has a time to end." We came out of our barracks to the yard as usual. We saw something different this time, however. We had look-out towers with SS soldiers in them, armed with machine guns. This morning, however, no one was in the look-out towers and there were no machine guns. We then heard shots outside of the gate, and all of a sudden the gates of Buchenwald opened ... We saw tanks coming in, soldiers with guns and jeeps. We thought they were going to level the entire camp and kill all of us, but we found out, however, they were American soldiers from General Patton's brigade. They came to save us ... to give us our lives back ... and I mean this literally. If these soldiers would have come a month later, there would not have been any survivors. We were all very sick, we were skin and bone, dead people walking.

I always say that thousands of years ago, God sent Moses and his brother Aaron to Egypt, to the King Pharaoh, to take the Jews out of slavery ...

AND IN APRIL OF 1945, GOD SENT THE AMERICAN ARMY, LED BY GENERAL PATTON, TO TAKE THE JEWS OUT OF SLAVERY ... THOSE SOLDIERS WERE LED BY GOD AND MOSES ... THE SOLDIERS WERE ANGELS OF GOD!

I heard and saw about twenty feet from me, what sounded like singing, crying, praying. I went closer; I saw that an American soldier had been lifted up in the air by some very weak Jewish prisoners. They were dancing with him, crying with him, praying with him. If you could visualize this picture ... you would remember this scene for your entire life.

I found out that this American soldier was Jewish and a rabbi. His name was Herschel Schacter, a Chaplain of the

Third Division of General Patton's unit.

Rabbi Schacter led us in prayer services. This was the first time we were able to say the mourner's kaddish for all the people murdered in the Holocaust – our parents, brothers, sisters, husbands, wives – our six million martyrs.

This was the first time we saw people could see our broken hearts ... Within a few hours, we had ambulances with doctors, nurses, medicine and food. But we were told we could not eat too much food. Our bodies could not handle food yet, and we could possibly die from eating too much.

Four of us would lay down to sleep in a wooden frame on any night ... but not all four of us would be alive in the morning to get up. Each barrack had dead people outside of the door. Some had five, some had ten. When the Americans saw this, they called in the mayor of the closest city, which was Weimar, and asked him what had happened here. The

Liberation of the Buchenwald Concentration Camp by the 6th Armored Division of US Third Army, April 11, 1945.

Rabbi Herschel Schacter conducts Shavuot services in liberated Buchenwald.

mayor said he didn't know.

On Sunday, April 15, 1945, CBS radio news reporter Edward R. Murrow broadcast his first-hand account of what he had seen at Buchenwald on April 12th, the day after the concentration camp was liberated by the American troops.

The title of Edward R. Murrow's radio broadcast was "They Died 900 a Day in 'the Best' Nazi Death Camp." One of the prisoners in the camp had told him that in 1939 when Polish prisoners arrived in the camp without winter clothing, they died at the rate of 900 per day. Five different men in the camp, who had experience in other Nazi camps, said that Buchenwald was the best of all the camps.

This is how Murrow's broadcast began ...

> *During the last week, I have driven more than a few hundred miles through Germany, most of it in the Third Army Sector ... Wiesbaden, Frankfurt, Weimar, Jena and*

beyond ... Permit me to tell you what you would have seen, and heard, had you been with me on Thursday. It will not be pleasant listening. If you are at lunch, or if you have no appetite to hear what the Germans have done, now is a good time to switch off the radio for I propose to tell you of Buchenwald...

With Murrow's reports, and the photographs of the American Army, the world began to understand the atrocities that the Germans had committed.

The American Army said they would take 1,000 children from Buchenwald and send them by plane to New York. I was fortunate to qualify for this "age group" but I told them, "I don't want to go to New York at this time." You see, my mother, who was born in 1901, in 1945 was only 44 years old. My father, who was born in 1896, was only 49 years old. Although I had seen the gas chamber and the crematoriums and smelled what was rising from the chimneys, I didn't

The liberated children of Buchenwald are escorted out of the camp by the American Army.

believe that my parents were not alive. I wanted to go home and search for them. I thought to myself, "Hitler is dead, and the three of us would decide where we would spend the rest of our lives."

For those of us who wanted to go to Czechoslovakia or Hungary, the American Army took us to Prague, to the railroad station. I found many survivors from all over Europe. I found a woman who came from our hometown in Kaszony, who knew all of us very well. She asked me what I was going to do. I told her I wanted to go home and search for my parents.

This woman told me not to search for my mother. She said my mother was standing near her during selections. She was sent by the Nazi soldier to the right. All those who were sent to the right were sent directly to the gas chamber.

But I still had to search for my father. There were four of us from Kaszony who found each other and returned to our hometown together; myself, the woman who told me about my mother, and two other men. We had a hard time getting even a piece of bread there. The people did not want us there. I know the reason they didn't want us.

As I wrote earlier, there were many successful Jewish families in our village. These were the people who had the stores and offices. After we were deported, the Kaszony people divided all of the Jewish property. Some got the rich homes, the grocery store, the hardware store, everything the Jews owned, and they didn't want to give back what belonged to our families.

The four of us remembered the story in the Torah when God gave a piece of land to the Jewish people. He promised the land to our Patriarchs, Abraham, Isaac and Jacob. We decided that we would go to the Promised Land. The deed to the land is written in the Bible.

Our village was liberated by the Russians, so we had to go to the West. I went to Romania ... and coming into Bucharest, the first delicatessen I saw, I went and smelled the food. I had some coins in my pocket, I don't remember what kind of coins or where I got them ... I put it down on the counter ... I just pointed to the Mamoliga. (In Romania, one of their main dishes is Mamoliga, which was made from corn meal).

I still had my blue-striped uniform on. A Jewish man came to me and spoke to me in Yiddish, and asked me if I would like to have some soup. I said sure. Then another man came to me and asked if I would like a hamburger. Another man then came to me and asked me if I wanted a piece of cake. Then someone came and said to the waiter, "don't give him anymore." He saw that I didn't like that! He told me I could get very sick ... that I should come as long as I am in Bucharest, that I should come every night to eat by him. He lived across the street from the restaurant. And I did go every night!

One night after I finished dinner, the lady of the house asked if I wanted some more. When I said yes, their little girl, about eight years old, was kind enough to go to the refrigerator and bring more food. I have always dreamed of meeting this little girl ... I know she would be in her 80s today. I remember that her father was a dentist.

In the whole week that I was in Bucharest I was invited for breakfasts, lunches and dinners. Then I found out there was a Jewish organization there, called "The Joint," short for "The Joint Distribution Committee." I went there and I was given some money. I told them I wanted to go to Palestine. They told me to go to Budapest and they could help me there.

I started to make my way to Budapest by going to the railroad station. There was no room inside the train, so I climbed on top of the train. In the morning I was soaking wet ... and what little money I received from the Joint was gone. As I looked down, I saw the pocket of my pants was cut open.

After arriving in Budapest, I was told that I could stay in a public school building. It was called Erzsebet public school. Then, a few days later, I found out that my cousin Irene Herskovic was in another school building. I went and found my first relative who survived. This was a very happy occasion. We talked and cried together! Then, in the same week, I found another cousin from Kisdobrony who survived. Together we figured out that we had fifty-one family members and only the three of us survived.

When I went to visit my cousin Irene, she had a roommate, also a survivor by the name of Lili. We became good friends. After four weeks in Budapest, we were transferred to Austria, to the city called Wels.

We were assigned to a place in an old Army barrack, and again, the Joint and the American Army fed us and took care of our medical needs. Then I went to the consulate and told them that I wanted to go to Palestine. I showed them my papers from Auschwitz and Buchenwald. I told the consulate that I returned to my home where I lived before, and the Hungarian government had forced me, my family and the Jewish people out of our homes.

"Today I am homeless and have no place to live," I told them. "I want to go to Palestine, to the 'Promised Land,' our God-given country." They told me that anyone could go to Palestine, except someone Jewish, so I stayed in Wels.

Then winter came and they took us to the city of Bad Gastin, which was a resort city. I was placed in the Hotel Austria. Then again the Joint and the American Army gave me support.

I married the lady whom I met through my cousin Irene. Our wedding was held in the same hotel where we lived. The chef of the hotel who prepared our meals prepared a very nice kosher dinner. I bought one full bottle of whiskey. Soon I had to buy another one. For that, I had to borrow some money. My suit and shirt were also borrowed. My bride's wedding gown was also borrowed. By the way, this wedding gown was a used wedding gown and was sent to our camp from America. Twenty-five girls got married in that wedding gown and not one of these women ever got divorced!

The United States of America

My new bride found an old Hungarian newspaper and wrote to the editor that she was trying to locate her uncle in America, whose name was Sam Hirsch, a baker. She didn't know his address, however. They printed her letter and amazingly, someone who read that paper knew her uncle and helped us get in contact with him. Her uncle arranged the documents we needed to come to the United States of America. We arrived in Fairmont, West Virginia and were greeted and entertained by the whole community. We were the only Holocaust survivors in the community.

I told my new uncle that I wanted to go to work. He said, "Don't worry, you will work enough in America ... I know of a dry cleaner where I take my clothes and he is always looking for help." I got the job! I worked 5½ days and got paid $30.00. I was the happiest man in Fairmont, West Virginia!

I was an only child, but my wife had eight brothers and sisters. One of her sisters was also a survivor. Her name was Sarah. She got married before we were sent to the ghetto. A few months later, her husband was drafted into the forced labor unit and later died in that unit. She was pregnant at the time and gave birth to a boy. They had a very good friend ... a Christian who had a farm, and he hid her and her little boy during the war.

While hiding children with Christian families to save their lives was permitted by most Rabbis, some Jews refused. They said "we do not know when we will be obligated to return our deposit to Hashem, to our God, but one thing we are sure of, and certain of, is that we will return the souls of our children as Jews."

After liberation, the Joint sent Sarah and her son to Detroit, Michigan. At that point, we hadn't seen very many Jewish children after the war because so many of our youth had been murdered in the Holocaust. The two sisters wanted to be together, so we moved to Detroit. We came to Detroit on January 1, 1950 and I found a job at a dry cleaner as a presser. Many survivors arrived in Detroit around that time.

Before I left Fairmont, I thanked our aunt and uncle for welcoming us into their home, especially me, since, in a way, I was a stranger. They treated us as their own children. Soon after we left for Detroit, they moved to Miami Beach, Florida. They told us that we should move to Miami, so I visited them and looked for a job, but I just couldn't find one!

Our dear uncle died first. We went to the funeral. And then we went to the funeral of our dear aunt. God should take care of you, you beautiful, wonderful people.

I read this poem at the funeral of my Aunt Etta:

God saw she was getting tired
And a cure was not to be,
So He put His arms around her
And whispered come with Me.

With tearful eyes we watched her suffer
And saw her fade away.
Although we loved her dearly,
We could not make her stay.

A golden heart stopped beating.
Hard working hands to rest.
God broke our hearts to prove to us
He only takes the best.

Those of us in Detroit who came from Hungary and Czechoslovakia formed a survivors' organization which we called the United Jewish Organization. We were learning to speak English and many didn't have jobs. Together, we tried to plan our future. The first thing we did together as an organization was put up a memorial stone for our parents.

The matsevahs that we dedicated in Detroit to remember our family members who were murdered in the Holocaust.

Gratitude To My New Country

Coming to this country ... which was a blessing from God Himself, has to be like coming from Hell to Heaven. America gave us a home when we had none. We were homeless and had nothing and nobody. America embraced us when we were rejected by the whole world. It gave us a feeling that we belonged.

I came from a DP camp in Bad Gastin, which identified us as Displaced Persons. Today the letters "DP" identify us as "Delayed Pilgrims." We are proud to be Americans.

My profession during my life in America was the dry cleaning business. I cleaned American flags; I cleaned the uniforms of American soldiers.

I want to say to America and to the American Government, thank you for all you have done for us Holocaust survivors and the good you continue to do for the entire world. God bless America.

With much gratitude, I remember the soldiers of the United States of America and the Allied soldiers who fought to defeat the Nazi enemy, and who eventually liberated me from Buchenwald.

One day, I would like to go to Pearl Harbor before I get too old, and bow my head, and say a prayer of "Thank You" to those brave American soldiers who died there, too.

The Obligation To Remember

Our six million martyrs includes our fathers and mothers, our people. They never had a funeral ... or even a grave.

As we know, everyone dies. If a father or mother dies ... the children, the family... have a funeral. There is a grave. We sit "shiva" for seven days. We don't go out from our house ... we say prayers. But for our six million martyrs who were murdered during the Holocaust in Europe and then burned in crematoriums, they never had a funeral, there is no grave

I participated in the candle-lighting ceremony to remember all the people murdered in the Holocaust.

or marker. Their graves are in Heaven and in our hearts.

We dedicated a memorial stone with the names of our parents and grandparents ... our families' names on it, in English and in Yiddish. The memorial stone to mark the grave is called the "matsevah." For the six million martyrs ... they have no matsevahs.

Our organization, twice a year, holds a Yahrzeit memorial remembrance for the people who were murdered in the Holocaust. We have a gathering in which we light six candles to honor the six million martyrs who were killed in Auschwitz, Buchenwald, Bergen Belsen, Dachau, Treblinka, Maydenek and all the other concentration camps.

We survivors are less and less each year. We think the history of the Holocaust shouldn't die with us but should be remembered. For that, we will need the continued support and participation as well as attendance to our Yizkor services from the second and third generation of survivors.

The Yahrzeit Of My Father

Throughout our history, we the Jewish people have had a custom to go and pray at the graves of parents, grandparents, family members and great rabbis, especially on the holy days before and during the High Holidays. We also visit the grave on the day when we observe a yahrzeit. I observe my father's yahrzeit on the first day of Rosh Hashana.

Neither my father or my mother or the six million Jews murdered in the Holocaust ever had a funeral service, and most do not have a grave in a cemetery. There is no place to got to and say prayers. There is no matsevah.

I remember the day in the evening when we came from the factory in Zeitz where I worked with my father. Together we stood in line to be counted as usual. The German officers went through the lines and they told those whom they thought were too weak to work that they would be sent to Buchenwald, to a hospital for rest. But later, I found out the Germans never sent a Jew to a hospital to rest.

I would like to tell my children a few words about their Zeidy. He grew up in the Carpathians without a father. Your great grandfather was killed in the first World War.

Zeidy had a reputation for being kind and generous. He was a "Mensh." He loved his family, and worked very hard as a tailor. Many times your Bubby helped him.

The neshamas (souls) of Zeidy and Bubby are down here and they have nachas (joy and happiness) from all of your learning in Yeshivot. Let's wish all the neshamas a good Yuntuf.

Our children, our grandchildren ... let them come to this Yizkor service to learn what their parents, grandparents and extended family went through ... to encourage them to attend. We need them to attend because they are the future generations. They must never forget! We need active participation from the entire local Jewish community. We need leadership from the rabbis. It should be taught in the classrooms.

The candles represent our holy synagogues, our holy Torahs which were burned to ashes. We also light a candle as well for those people who survived the Holocaust, but have since died as well as the fallen soldiers who gave up their lives fighting against anti-Semitism and Nazism.

These candles memorialize all the holy rabbis, our teachers who taught us and led us and sometimes encouraged us until their tragic end. Also the candles represent all of the Freedom Fighters who were killed in the forest of Nazi Germany.

The candles also represent the children whose voices were silenced, whose lives were cut short, whose future was never fulfilled ... who never went to "cheder" (Hebrew school) who never stood under the marriage "chuppah."

Jewish life has always revolved around the family, with children being the focal point.

In my parents' home, children were always treasured. I remember at dinner, if there was something which I liked, and said so, immediately I heard my mother (God bless her soul) say, "I'm not that hungry, have some of mine." Then my father (God bless his soul) would also say, "I'm not that hungry either, have some of mine."

By the time World War II ended, the Jewish children of Europe, 1,500,000 children were murdered in gas chambers and burned in crematoriums.

So when I recently read an article in "The Jewish Press" (July 10, 2015) by Rebbetzin Esther Jungreis, who is also a survivor of the concentration camps, it reminded me that

Hashem has plan that is not yet known to us.

In her article, she tells the story of how at Mount Sinai, when Hashem gave us the holy Torah, he asked for guarantors to ensure that the Torah would not be forgotten. Many suggestions were offered. Our patriarchs and our matriarchs and our prophets were offered. But Hashem would not accept these giants in our faith as guarantors. Then someone said, "Let our children be the guarantors." Hashem accepted immediately this suggestion. And so our children have been the guarantors of our Torah throughout the generations.

When I showed the article to my son, he quoted the Gemara in tractate Shabbat, which says, "The world continues to exist only in the merit of the words that come from the mouths of children as they study the Torah.

Our small Jewish organization accomplished many good things! We bought over thirty (30) cemetery plots ("chessed shel emet") in the Jewish cemetery. We sold these plots to our members for the same price in which we bought them. We bought a forest of trees in Jerusalem in our name at the Kennedy Forest. By now, I estimate we have about 20,000 trees of ours in there. Together, we assisted the State of Israel with our successful bond drive. (We were paid back after its maturity with interest.) We contributed to the Jewish organization, The Joint. It is the same organization that helped us when we were in need in Europe.

Our Family

In the meantime, we found out we were expecting a child. Our first son, Arthur, was born on July 22, 1950. You can imagine going through the concentration camps and being without parents ... and know you have your own son ... how happy we were on one hand, but on the other hand, it would've been nice to have his grandmother and grandfather here. That young man today is now my older son, 65 years old and works as a lawyer in Farmington Hills and is a proud parent of four children. God blessed him throughout his life. We named him Arthur after my father (who was killed in the Holocaust), so his name should continue.

In September of 1960, we had another child whom we named Mark. Today, he is a Rabbi and the father of six children. Mark was named after his mother's grandfather and great-grandfather (who were killed in The Holocaust), so his name could continue. Mark has six children of his own today, three of whom are married. He is the proud grandfather of six children. He has been teaching Hebrew and Mathematics at Yeshiva Beth Yehuda for 30 years (which

On the wedding of our granddaughter and grandson: Standing (L-R): My son Arthur, his son Logan, me, my grandson Chuny, my granddaughter Chana, my wife Lilly, my grandson Devin. Seated: My son Mottel and his wife Jackie.

Back Row (L-R) My wife Lilly, me, my son Mottel, his wife Jackie, my grandson Moshe. Front Row (L-R) My grandchildren: Esther, Dovid, Yossi, Avi and Chana.

Our granddaughter, Layne.

With granddaughter, Taylor.

was the only job he's ever had!). He enjoys this very much and I am very proud of him!

Coming to Detroit we were looking for a Rabbi who would do the circumcision for our son. Someone had told me there was a young couple who came from Poland, both of whom had been in concentration camps and in the Russian Army. His name was Rabbi Leo Goldman. We struck up a friendship which lasted for 65 years until his passing. He was a very good friend. In a way, we became like family. He was Arthur's "mohel," the one who did the circumcision. Even his children, grandchildren and great-grandchildren consider us as family. His son-in-law, Henry Brystowsky, is my doctor and friend. Rabbi Goldman's daughter, whose name is Reizel, I see regularly in the synagogue on Saturdays. God bless the

My rabbi, Rabbi Leo Goldman.

memory of my great friend Rabbi Leo Goldman. His other daughter, Vivian, told me she used to call her father every Friday afternoon before the Sabbath. Now she's calling me every Friday afternoon!

My wife, Lili, and I were happily married and lived together for 33 years. Unfortunately she became ill, and after being ill for five years, she passed away. My first son Arthur was engaged at this time and we had to postpone his wedding. Our entire family was shocked by my wife's death.

Our grandchild Brandon was born with aplastic anemia, his bone marrow did not produce enough blood cells. May he rest in peace and God bless his soul.

Remembering my first wife and our grandson Brandon.

I was alone for five and a half years and then I was introduced to my soon to be second wife. I am not sure who introduced us … Was it Erzsi Stein? Was it Hedy Duschinsky? I know that one of you did, and I thank you very much for that, first of all.

Hedy told me there was a young lady in Youngstown, Ohio whom I should meet. I went to Youngstown, and when we talked. We discovered that we had many things in common. She didn't have parents, I didn't have parents either. She had two children, I had children. Her name was Lilly … that was the name of my first wife. Her first husband's name was Michael, which is the same as mine! Her maiden name was Weiss, which is the same last name as mine! We got married 32 years ago … Her birthday is June 7, which is the same day I arrived to the United States. (It is the week of June 7, 2015 as I write this!) Our destiny to be with each other was fulfilled as determined in Heaven.

Our wedding celebration.

Lilly Weiss Is Also A Survivor

My husband is Michael Weiss, the author of this book. I am also a Holocaust survivor. When he began writing this book about his experiences during the Holocaust, he asked me if I would write some of my experiences during my time in the Holocaust. For me, it is not an easy task to talk or write about it. I will try my best to tell you my story.

Jews first settled in Balassagyarmat, a city in northern Hungary near the border of Slovakia, toward the end of the 17th century. I was born there in 1930 to Lenke Slomovits and Ignacz Weisz. I have an older sister Edith, born in 1927, and two younger brothers, Gyorgy and Josef.

My father, Ignacz, owned a small shoe store and my mother, Lenke was a good cook and baker. We lived in walking distance to my mother's parents, Rosa and Sandor Slomovits. My grandparents had eleven children, nine girls and two boys. All their children went to a Jewish school and we had a beautiful Jewish life in Balassagyarmat. I can still remember picking up the cholent for Shabbos from the kosher bakery which you could smell from far away. It's nice to remember those little things that Jewish people kept in Europe.

We were a happy family until the tragedy began. The Germans came and put us in the ghettos and then transferred us to a place on the outskirts of Balassagyarmat that used to be a factory for drying tobacco (Nyirjespuszta). It was a small place with no side walls or roof. There were babies and old people there. It was a terrible place.

My father had been sent to forced labor camp in a city named Nagcenk on the border of Hungary and Germany. I heard later that just a few days or few weeks before the liberation, he and the others were shot and supposed to be

Lilly's father,
Ignacz Weisz.

Lilly's mother,
Lenke Slomovits Weisz.

buried in a mass grave.

After two weeks in Nyirjes, my mother, sister, brothers, grandparents and I were transported to Auschwitz in cattle cars (boxcars). We were squeezed in like sardines with no bathroom, no food and no water. It was terrible to see my grandfather standing in one place and just staring out the small window of the cattle car. When we arrived in Auschwitz, everything went so fast. The Germans had dogs which were barking and jumping on us and we were very scared. I remember that my grandmother stepped down from the train and she was crying and touched each grandchild.

My mother was 36 years old and I remember she was holding the hands of my two younger brothers. That was the last time I saw them. My sister, Edith and I were sent to a building and ordered to take off our clothes. We folded them up neatly thinking when we came back we would put them back on and we would wear them again. Of course we never went back on that side of the building. They also cut our hair and Edith and I held hands because we were afraid that we would not recognize each other. They gave me a burgundy/ reddish colored dress with short sleeves. On the back of the

The Slomovits family in Hungary.
Lilly's grandparents with great uncles and great aunts.
Front row, second from left:
Lilly's grandmother (died in Auschwitz).
Front row, third from left:
Lilly's grandfather (died in Auschwitz).
End of front row: Lilly's mother.

Synagogue in Balassagyarmat.

dress there was one black stripe. That is what we wore in Auschwitz.

When they lined us up to be counted, Dr Mengele came and always separated Edith and me. Then we learned not to stand behind each other. Many thought that Mengele recognized those that were related. We heard about Mengele's experiments with twins while we were in Auschwitz and learned a lot more after the war from the shochet in Balassagyarmat, Mr. Braun. He had twin grandchildren, one of which did not survive.

Everybody worried if they were going to gas us because we saw what was happening when we came to Auschwitz. We saw the smoke coming from the chimney and we asked our blockova (barracks leader) what that was. I remember that she said that it was our parents and the others that came with us to Auschwitz and they were probably dead.

After three months they transferred us to Bergen-Belsen. It was awful there. We did not have water or food there. It was terrible. There were rats all over and my sister and I were very scared. When we were lying down to sleep, we could hear the rats scratching and we were screaming. I still can't go into the garage today without knocking on the wall because I am so scared that rats or mice will be there.

Three months later, we were transferred to Aschersleben in Germany. While we were there we worked in an airplane factory. I was only 14 years old. My sister Edith and I worked on the side of the plane. Our job was to seal the bolts with a luft gun (air gun). It was very hard for us since the air gun was so heavy and it was jumping all over. The Germans checked our work and we were afraid that we would get in trouble for a bad job.

After another 3½ months, we were sent to Theresienstadt. We took a train partially and walked the rest of the way. We were walking and if you could not walk, they would shoot you. We saw many people dead by the road. My sister and

I were leaning on each other to help us to keep walking. If I wanted to sit down, my sister would tell me not to. If she couldn't walk anymore, I told her to please get up. The sole of my wooden shoes were totally missing. I saw my sister taking a pair of wooden shoes off a dead person for me to wear. My feet were bloody so I finally agreed to put the dead person's shoes on. We walked so far and everyone felt that we were in a death march. We arrived in Theresienstadt, which is in Czechoslovakia. We were there about three months and it was horrible there, awful!

In the spring of 1945, we were liberated by Russian soldiers. Our cousin, Ezra Moskovitz was a Czechoslovak soldier and he found us there. We were hungry, tired and very sick. He brought food for us and some other people and then he disappeared. Many years later, at a Hungarian gathering in Israel, I found out that he was alive and lived in Israel. So we found him and it was heartwarming to see him.

After a few months, in 1945, we got on a train and eventually arrived in Budapest where we found two surviving aunts (my mother's sisters – Szidi and Ilonka). We decided to go back to our hometown of Balassagyarmat. We still could not believe that our family, my mother and little brothers were killed, burned in Auschwitz. We were hoping to find them but that was not to be. We didn't have any clothes and we did not have any food. Nobody asked us to come in to have a slice of bread or something to eat. The gentiles didn't care and in a way they did not want us back because of what happened. They took everything that was left in their possession. One person may have taken the furniture and another house. They got everything that we left. We did not even have a chance to close or lock the door.

We were among the first ones who came back and we found some cousins, Bela Weisz and his son. We lived in a couple rooms at their house. Slowly other people came back and the Jewish community started a congregation and held meetings.

We got jobs and started to earn a living in Balassagyarmat. My sister married and had two sons. I married my brother-in-laws brother, Michael Aronovich (later changed to Aron when we became U.S. citizens). We had a son, George and a daughter, Eva.

Almost all the young women who had been in Auschwitz had a miscarriage or something went wrong with their first pregnancy. They gave us something to drink like black coffee that was very bitter. It was a medicine called broom and it stopped our monthly menstrual cycle. This medicine caused something to happen to our first pregnancy for almost all of us.

In 1957, when the Russians came to Hungary, my husband and I decided that we did not want to raise children there anymore. So we had to sneak out of Hungary. The plan was to go to the United States.

There is nothing like the United States. Two men agreed to help us all the way to Austria. It was winter and snowing. I was holding my son's hand and my husband was carrying my daughter. All of a sudden I looked up and they had disappeared. We could not see which way they went. I saw footsteps both ways and did not know which way to go. First we went to the left and then I said no, we are going to the right. We chose the right route. My husband begged them to stop and offered them more money to look for us. The men refused because there were many others with us also sneaking out. We walked and also took a train. While on the train we had to give the children a small dosage of sleeping pills so they would not cry.

When we arrived in Vienna, Austria, we did not have any strength whatsoever. We finally found a hotel for people who snuck out of Hungary to Austria. We did not have any papers so we did not know who was going to give us visas. We had to stay in Vienna for almost a year. It wasn't easy! At the end we found we had two non-Jewish friends in the

R-L: Lilly and her sister Edith.

United States that we had helped with some amount of money for them to go to the United States. They never forgot that we helped them and wanted to help us. They went to an attorney and found out we were in Austria. They told the attorney that we were very nice people and wanted to help us get to the United States. The attorney helped us obtain our visas.

Meanwhile, Edith's husband had both Hungarian and Czechoslovak citizenship and was able to go to the United States with regular papers on the quota for Czechoslovaks. So they also came to Austria first, but did not have to sneak out, and then to the U.S.

We settled in Youngstown, Ohio where our sponsors and attorney lived. We started a small fruit store business. Later we opened a grocery store. My sister Edith and her family also lived in Youngstown and our children grew up together like they were brothers and sister instead of cousins.

After my husband, Michael passed away, I had to get a job outside of the home. I worked in a department store, in the ladies clothing department. It was difficult working and raising teenagers.

Years later I met my second husband, Michael Weiss, who was also a survivor. He was from Kaszony, Czechoslovakia and currently living in the Detroit area. He has two sons, Arthur and Mark and between them, there were 13 grandchildren.

For me, it's been very hard. There is not a day that goes by that I don't think about my family. I was only 14 years old and my sister Edith was 17 years old. We did not have a childhood. I am 85 years old now and it hurts me that I don't remember if I ever said I love you mom or I love you dad. I have to only assume that I did. I did not have a chance since our childhood was stolen from us.

In Youngstown, we were busy with our lives and raising our children. But now that we are older, it's even worse. It saddens me that the children did not know their grandparents. They used to go to birthday parties and come home and say that the grandparents were there, and then ask me where

Linsay Aron, our granddaughter.

are their grandparents? The holidays came and went with no grandparents. It was very hard for the children, the second generation who still feel saddened today. They ask a lot of questions. The why is there for them all the time. It still hurts deeply, but I never talked about it to my children much as they were growing up because I didn't want to make their lives sad and give them nightmares. If they ask questions now, I try to talk to them and answer.

Jordan Aron, our grandson passed away from a type of cancer called rhabdomyosarcoma (RMS) at the age of 14. We were all very happy on the day of Jordan's Bar Mitzvah. He had a love for the Jewish religion – the customs and laws. When he came to visit us in Detroit it was always a happy occasion. He loved walking with me to shul. May he rest in peace. He is missed by all of our family.

Although it is hard for me to explain or try to describe what I went through in the Holocaust, my girlfriends and I talk about it almost daily. We are very lucky that we were able to cope through everything. All these years we're alive and were able to raise children, work and we are still here.

Sometimes I think about how so many people were gassed, burned, and how is it my sister and I managed to come back. My sister and I were so young, only 14 and 17. It's just unbelievable how much we went through at a young tender age and we survived. What helped Edith and I to survive was being together. That's how we survived. It's a miracle, it's really a miracle.

I still have hard feelings about the Hungarian people because they could have stood by the Jews and stated to the Germans that Hungary was their country. They could have fought with them, but they didn't. I remember walking down the street as a child and a young boy bumped into me and said, "You dirty Jew." You cannot forget something like this. They learn this at home. This boy and I used to play together.

As for the Germans, although I know that the younger generation is not responsible for what their grandfathers did, I cannot forgive the German people for what happened.

My message to the future generations is, don't ever forget! G-d forbid! This should never happen again. Don't forget, remember what the European Jewish people went through in the Holocaust. Remember how many people were burned and gassed in the gas chambers. Stop the hate here and in Israel too. We are good people.

Some people like me have a hard time talking about what happened because we lived through it. I choke on my tears, but please talk about it. The world should know what happened with the European Jews. Hitler tried to kill us all but for some miracles, he was not successful!

Don't ever forget!

A Second Generation Survivor

My name is Eva Aron, and I am a second generation Holocaust survivor. I have been asked to write a little information about me. I live in Tampa, Florida and I have one son, Michael named after my father and he is married to Melissa. I also have two wonderful grandchildren, a girl, Kailey who is nine years old and a boy, Jacob who is seven years old.

Michael Weiss, the author of this book, and my mother, Lilly Weiss, met and married 32 years ago. My brother and I have been very happy to have him in our lives.

My brother, George, being five years older than me, remembers the Russian tanks on the road when he came home from school. In fear of another Holocaust, my family snuck out of Hungary and went to Vienna. I was three years old when my blessed father, mother, brother and I escaped from Hungary when the Russians came.

Back: Michael Aron, Melissa.
Front: Kailey, Jacob.

As I was a baby, I don't remember the year we spent in Vienna waiting until we were sponsored so that we could come to the United States. The earliest recollection I have is sitting on the plane next to my father and the stewardess showing me a pillow as if to ask if I wanted it.

I remember arriving to Youngstown, Ohio, and

R-L: Lilly and Eva.

going outside to play and coming home crying that I did not understand what the little neighbor girls were saying. But it did not take long and as children are fast learners, I was soon speaking English. My parents wanted us to speak English to them so they could learn too.

My parents did not talk about the Holocaust to us because they did not want us to be saddened about the tragedy. My father was the kindest man I ever met. He never raised his voice or hand to us. Later my mother said he was just so happy to have survived and lived to have children. Everything and anything we did was all right with him. His untimely death when I was only 13 years old has affected me my entire life.

The first person that spoke about the Holocaust was my uncle, my father's brother. He was already older by then and so was I. When he opened up, we all started asking questions. I had a lot of questions which my mother answered and I heard her horrific story. Can you imagine that she lost her parents and was in a labor camp at the age of 14! How my parents survived is a true miracle.

As an adult, I remember a group of 15 or so friends went to see the movie, "Schindler's List" when the

George and Wendy Aron,
our son and daughter-in-law.

L-R: George Aron, me, Lilly and Eva Aron.

movie first came out. My cousin, Les, and I cried throughout the entire movie. After the movie was over and we could actually compose ourselves and speak, we both said that we pictured our parents there throughout the entire movie.

The next day I asked my mother if she saw the movie and she said she had. I asked her how was she able to watch it. I cried hysterically throughout the entire movie. I will never forget her answer to me. She said to her it was just a movie. The truth was that it was 100 times worse in real life when it actually happened! I thought about what she said and realized that Steven Spielberg did a great job with the movie based on facts. If he made it any sadder no one would have been able to watch it, but to my mother it did not depict one iota of all that truly happened!

My mother is the kindest, most generous and most loving person I have ever known. How she survived the cruelty of the Holocaust is a true miracle.

I tell her every day that I love her. And I am blessed to have her as my best friend!

To Remember And Remind

At the end of the war we found out that the Nazi government killed ... murdered ... six million of our dearest possessions. They killed our fathers, mothers; our little children ... The world heard the screams of our children after their mother. God heard the prayers of the six million martyrs from the gas chambers and crematoriums where they killed them ... where they burned them.

Our holy Torahs were destroyed and our holy synagogues were burned and destroyed. Our lives were destroyed in a very tragic way. But, God blessed us. He chose us to survive the Holocaust, to establish a new family, a new generation of children. We named them after our parents, after our families, whose names live on. And our children take part in our "Yizkor" (memorial) services. They will remember and will teach their children.

We remember all those victims for whom the borders were closed and they couldn't escape and ended up in the gas chambers and crematoriums.

Auschwitz is the most cursed piece of real estate in the whole universe. Auschwitz is not only the largest Jewish graveyard in the world, but also the largest mass-murder location in human history. The war against us, the Jewish people, started with burning our holy books and ended up with murdering over six million innocent Jewish people.

At the end of the Second World War, we the Jewish people didn't stop suffering. Many died from exhaustion, irreversible sickness and malnutrition ... In the hospitals of Germany and Austria, in Displaced Persons camps and on their way to look for a new home in Palestine, Hungary, Czechoslovakia, the United States or any country in the world that might be willing to accept them. Some had survived concentration camps, labor camps, prisoner of war camps, partisan camps and the various armies of the Allies. Many survived in large cities like Budapest, with false names and identity papers. All had a terrible story to tell. Their plight was extremely painful. There were no homes to return to, no families to rely on for help.

Many of the non-Jews were hostile and still poisoned by racial hatred. They were fearful of losing the Jewish loot they were hiding in the Jewish home in which they were living.

The great majority of Jews from our region who survived didn't return to Subcarpathia, but remained in the DP camps in Germany in the hope of reaching Palestine or the United States. Up to 8,000 moved westward to Czechoslovakia.

At luncheon, Holocaust survivors keep past alive

Holocaust survivor Michael Weiss (right) talks about his experiences with University Housing staff member Jeff Kenney during Hillel's Conference on the Holocaust. The annual event brings in survivors to talk with University community leaders.

This article appeared in the newspaper.

Remembering The Holocaust On Yom Kippur

The first month of the Jewish year, Tishrei is also the holiest month of the year. On the Yom Tov of Rosh Hashana, God writes in the Book of Life for the coming year as we say in our prayers: "Who will live, who will die, who by fire, who by water, who by hunger, who by thirst, who by stoning, who by strangling..."

We, the Jewish people of Europe, had a very bad verdict in the six years between 1939 and 1945. The Hamans and then the Pharaohs - the anti-Semites - killed Your people, Ribbono Shel Olam, by fire, by water, by hunger, by stoning and by strangling. And by gas chambers. They killed Jewish people because they were Jewish. Then they were taken to the crematoriums where they were burned to ashes. They burned our Beis Hamikdash, they burned our Torahs.

After liberation we found out that the Nazis had murdered six million Jews. One and a half million children were murdered. All what was left from European Jewish life was ashes and cemeteries.

Europe is the continent that destroyed Jewish tradition and Europe is the continent that destroyed Jewish life. Every inch of the European continent is cursed because it is soaked with Jewish blood. Every silent barrack from hundreds of concentration camps over Europe is crying out about the six million victims who were murdered.

Seventy years after liberation, the experience from the Holocaust still hurts. It is like a cancer which never heals. We can still hear their cries and feel their pain. As long as one of us survivors is alive, we will remember, never forget, the six million. The six million Kedoshim never had a funeral, never had a grave. Nobody sat shiva and nobody said kaddish for them.

Soon it will be Yom Kippur. We pray for forgiveness for the sins we committed and on Yom Kippur is mazkir neshamas and we remember our family members who died but after the churbin. We will remember the six million Kedoshim whose neshamas are down here with us, and we will say yizkor.

My article appeared in The Jewish Press.

Most of them went into towns in the Sudetenland area. A few settled in Budapest, others in countries of five continents. Some were able to resettle in their former places of residence.

Later, other Jews arrived from distant parts of the Soviet Union, mainly office workers and technical administrators employed by the Soviet state.

In the second half of 1970, the Soviets opened the doors for many to leave. Hundreds of families left for Israel, the United States and other countries of the world. Very few remained of the original population. In Kaszony, as far as it is known, there was only one family who remained ... the family of Karcsi Lebovics, who has since died.

After liberation when I returned to Kaszony, I went to our family's house and the shul, but I could not enter either place. There were Russian soldiers everywhere. I saw other houses of the Jewish families, but no Jewish people. It was years before I saw a Jewish child. Even today, 70 years later, when I see Jewish children, it makes me feel good. Could their families be from my hometown?

Deep in my *neshama*, I saw the suffering and the persecution of my family. I worked together with my father for about five months, and saw his suffering ... the beatings he got ... and I saw the suffering of the 4000 people who worked with me in building the factory that would make gasoline out of coal.

I feel the suffering of my six million brethren ... the cruelty and horror of Nazi Germany and the many volunteers for Hitler during the Holocaust years is deeply embedded in my mind. Because it is such a powerful event, it overshadows everything else. It will remain in my mind forever ... it is something that never heals.

I took it upon myself to remember and remind the world of those tragic years when the Germans conducted a systematic annihilation of our people ... to live in the present a simple, humble and modest life and to believe in the future of the Jewish people, especially after the establishment of the State of Israel. I pray to the Almighty in His conducting of the world, in His own time and in His own way, He will punish the nations and the people who participated in the persecution of His children, the Jewish people.

Years after living in the United States, I heard a well-educated Jewish man say that Hitler was a messenger from God. I was in shock. He made this up. There is no place in any of our holy books to lead to this statement. I will never believe this, nor can I ever forget it. I hope that there are not any people who would believe a statement like this!

During the early years when Hitler came to power, the Jews were caught unprepared. But this is not the case today! With a Jewish state and Jewish army, there is someone who will come to the rescue of Jews. As an example, in 1976, the Israeli Army rescued the Jews who were held hostage by hijackers from the Popular Front for the Liberation of Palestine in Entebbe, Uganda.

In the pre-Holocaust period, there were no Jewish organizations in America, Europe, Palestine or any place that had plans to save European Jewry. Only Vladimir Zev Jabotinski in the late 1930s called for Jews to leave eastern Europe for Palestine. His calls went unanswered. I don't think that even Jabotinski imagined that the catastrophe would be so severe! Who could imagine such atrocities?

In fact, there were Jewish leaders who said it was Jabotinski who would bring harm to the Jews. There was no plan to encourage Jews to fight back or try to derail Germany's ultimate "Final Solution" plan for the destruction of European Jewry.

Many times during the years I wondered how this happened. Is it possible one morning Hitler came into his office and said, "Gentlemen, I want to kill all the Jews in Germany." Then maybe someone on his staff said, "My fuhrer we will need lots of bullets and we will need lots of coffins to bury them." Another member must have said, "I am a chemical engineer. I can build a room large enough to hold thousands of them and fill it with poison gas to kill them. And I can build a furnace where we can burn their bodies to ashes." And yes their plan was fulfilled. In Auschwitz alone, they killed over a million people; most of these people were Jewish.

It still amazes me how the German government decided that the Jews were their enemy. We the Jewish people, who lived in Europe for almost 900 years, obeyed the laws of whatever country we lived in. We never wanted to take over a country. We never bombed a building. We paid more than our fair share of taxes. If we were called to war, we went. Both of my grandfathers fought in World War I in the Austro-Hungarian army. One from my father's side never came back because he was killed. But all of that was not enough proof of our allegiance. Then the Nazi governments of Europe, (because we know Hitler did not do this all by himself), took us out of our homes and put us into ghettos. They took us to concentration camps in Auschwitz, Buchenwald, Majdenek and Buna and many other camps. There we found their death factories equipped with gas chambers and crematoriums.

(During the years, many times when I came down with my wife for breakfast, we would listen to the radio or television and hear the tragic news that a child was killed, sometimes two or three. We never asked what religion the child was, what their color or race was ... it was a child who probably had a mother, father and family who were in mourning for their child, just like any other family. This made breakfast difficult to swallow.)

During the Holocaust, the Nazi government (between 1939 and 1945) murdered, in a premeditated manner, one and a half million (1,500,000!) innocent children. The Nazi government of Europe murdered six million (6,000,000!)

innocent Jewish people. These people were murdered just because they were Jewish.

And I say, "The bad people did this." So many nations prevented Jews from finding a haven in their country. But my question is ... "What were the good people doing? What were the Western countries doing ... including our beloved United States of America?" We the survivors, we the Jewish people, we love this country very much. But, for us, the borders of the United States, however, were closed.

The British Empire stood by and prevented Jews from entering British territory. The British published a white paper forbidding the Jews from entering Israel, Palestine at that time. They prevented Jewish immigrants from entering the land of Israel, our historic homeland. The British Navy was busy hunting down Jewish refugee boats when they should've been fighting Nazis. The rescue routes were blocked everywhere! The song We Ahin Zol Ich Gehn ("Tell me where I should go") which was composed during the Holocaust years tells it all. Only a handful of Jews were saved through miraculous ways and deeds.

I often think about what happened to the ship with one thousand Jewish passengers that departed from Germany, legally, with visas, sailing to Cuba. The ship's name was "MS St. Louis." Upon arrival, the Cubans did not let the passengers disembark. The ship's captain, a Christian, said to the people, "don't worry, we are not far from America. We will go to Florida and there you have a good friend, the President of the United States, Franklin D. Roosevelt, who loves the Jewish people." They came to the shores of Florida, but again were not allowed to disembark. How could the president not let these people ashore? The ship returned to Europe, and all the passengers disembarked in various countries, only to be caught up in the Holocaust. The captain brought an empty vessel back to Hamburg.

Israel – Our Homeland

Now Iran is building an atomic bomb and the free world doesn't allow Israel to build apartments! And I think they have atomic bombs already, because money will buy you anything. We the Jewish people are facing the worst worldwide outbreak of anti-Semitism since the 1930s. Europe and much of the rest of the world is infected with the virus of anti-Semitism and some countries are threatening genocide. Since we established Israel, which God gave to His people, we were attacked by Arab countries, by Hamas, Fatah, Hezbollah, Islamic Jihad and by many more. Israel has come under repeated rocket attacks and suicide bombers, killing innocent people in the streets, babies in their cribs and carriages, children in schools, rabbis in their synagogues.

We thought that only the cities of European Jews were in danger, but in our country, within our borders, we should feel secure in our safety.

A friend of mine whom I know from home currently living in Israel called me a few years ago. He said, "The Holocaust is not over yet." I said, "What do you mean?" He said, "You know my parents ... my family ... were killed in Auschwitz. And now my daughter was coming home from Jerusalem to Haifa on the bus ... An Arab suicide bomber blew up the bus. I had to pick the pieces of her body up and bury her. To me, it doesn't make a difference. They killed my parents ... now in my own country they killed my little girl."

Israel is the only democratic country in the Middle East. That small country is the most racially mixed in the Middle East. Arabs are about 20 percent of the population of Israel. They enjoy the same rights as Jews. All Arabs who live in Israel have voting rights. There are Arabs who are openly against Israel and are members of the Knesset, Israel's parliament. Some are diplomats representing Israel all over the world. Some are deputy speakers.

Arab students who live in Israel can go to study at Israeli universities. The needy receive subsidies for education (just like Israelis). The Middle East has twenty-three countries, twenty-two Arab countries with approximately two hundred million people. Israel has about eight million people.

The Middle East, territory-wise, is twice as big as the United States of America. It is very difficult to understand how they couldn't find room for five or six million Jews! The Middle East could be the nicest part of the world.

And that's what we Jews want. Leave this little land that we have in Israel right now to the Jews. I'm sure it is well-known by the Arabs and Muslims that we are relatives. Abraham had his first son named Ishmael. The Arabs and Muslims are descendants from Ishmael. If you look in our Holy Bible, the five books of Moses, you will find that the land of Israel, what God Himself gave to the Jewish people, is the birthplace of our people. Here our religion and spiritual identity was given. Here we achieved our independence. God wrote the Torah and gave it to Moses to pass along to us, the Jewish people.

My question is, "Why could we not live in peace?" We talk about peace ... all of our presidents since 1948 have tried to make peace and they couldn't.

I, Michael Weiss, a Holocaust survivor from Auschwitz, my number 57490, what I received in Buchenwald, can make peace very easily. Take a piece of paper and write on it, "We will not kill any more Jews."

The return after 3,000 years to our Jewish homeland in 1948 gave us, the Holocaust survivors, and the Jewish people around the world hope ... a country with our own president, army and police force. The Jewish people could feel safe within our country and borders. And we hope we will be able to live safely with these things. God bless us all.

On Friday the fifth day of Iyar 5708, May 14 1948, just a few hours before Shabbat began, the British mandate on Palestine was to expire. We listened to the Hagannah Radio Station when it was announced that the leader of the Yishuv, the Jewish community in Eretz Yisrael gathered in the assembly hall of Tel Aviv Museum. On the platform stood David Ben Gurion, the chairman of the provisional government.

In a Jewish voice, Ben Gurion began saying, "We the members of the people's counsel, representatives of the Jewish Community of Eretz Yisrael and the Zionist movement are here assembled on the day of the termination of the British mandate over Eretz Yisrael and by the virtue of our national and historic right, and on the basis of the resolution of the United Nations, hereby declare the establishment of

David Ben Gurion, flanked by the members of the new Israeli government, reads the Declaration of Independence.

a Jewish state in Eretz Yisrael, to be known as the State of Israel."

The 37 representatives of the Jewish community in Eretz Yisrael stepped forward, one after another and signed the Declaration of Independence. This announcement would never have happened were it not for years of yearning, praying, hard labor, pioneering and creativity which led to the building of cities, towns, villages making an isolated country once again into a flourishing land with the Hebrew language and culture.

Immediately after midnight on that Friday, May 15 1948, the Arabs openly declared war against the newborn state and ordered the armies of Egypt, Jordan, Iraq, Syria and Lebanon as well as units from other Arab countries to invade Eretz Yisrael. In the south, the Egyptians sent their regular Army with tanks, artillery, armored vehicles and all kinds of weapons. All around the country, the other Arab armies did the same. Their plan was to choke, and God forbid, to destroy the fledgling Jewish estate with a blitzkrieg and throw the Jews into the sea. The Jewish forces organized themselves quickly to repel the invasion.

Jerusalem

Three thousand years ago King David established Jerusalem as the capital of Israel. His son, King Solomon, built the first "Beit HaMikdash" (the Holy Temple) on Mount Moriah.

Jerusalem is the heart of the Jewish religion mentioned in the Torah 656 times. The Muslim Koran does not mention Jerusalem even once! Jerusalem is a Jewish city and the crown of Israel. It is our capital.

When Jews outside of Israel pray, they face east towards Jerusalem. In Israel, Jews pray in the direction of Jerusalem. From Haifa, they face south. In Eilat, they face north. In Jerusalem, Jews face "Har HaBayit" where the Temples once stood, when they pray.

I am lighting a candle in Jerusalem near Har Habayit in remembrance of the people from my town Kaszony. Behind me are plaques with the names of towns destroyed in the Holocaust.

Our patriarch, Abraham, brought his only son Isaac to be sacrificed on Mount Moriah, where the Temples where built. Let's hope and pray that we will have the "Geula Shelema Bimhayra Beyamaenu" (that we should see the real redemption in our time).

We know that our martyrs perished with a dream of Jerusalem. Today the Jewish people, including the survivors of the Holocaust, stand tall with Israel as the center of Jewish society, present and future. With pride, we treasure the miracle of our Jewish people reborn in the State of Israel, which became a reality in our generation. We remember all those who gave their lives in Israeli wars for freedom and security ... so many Holocaust survivors among them.

In Israel, I am standing at a memorial for the people who died in the Holocaust from Czechoslovakia, Hungary and Transylvania.

Legacy Of The Survivors

The world gathering of Jewish Holocaust survivors that was held in Israel, June 14-18, 1981, was one of the biggest events in Jewish history.

We, the Jewish survivors, gathered here from 23 countries ... we assembled in Israel on our 36th anniversary of liberation to bear witness and to proclaim the legacy for future generations. We have been part of a history too tragic and powerful for the outside world to fully comprehend. We met for the first time, with our fellow survivors from all over the world to celebrate survival and the rebuilding of life, to reaffirm the durability of the Jewish spirit and the continuity of the Jewish people with Israel as its focus.

We were the largest number of survivors ever assembled in one place since our liberation thirty-six years ago. All of us were united by an undividable bond, a bond forged in death camps in Nazi Germany, the ghettos of Poland, in the forests where we fought, in places where non-Jews kept us hidden and saved our lives. It was a reunion of a special group of people. At the gathering, we were strong, standing together in the land created of the ashes of our parents, families, friends, those known and those unknown ... six million of them killed because they were Jews.

To transmit the survivors' legacy to our children and all future generations, every survivor came to see, to hear and to be part of that great, dramatic event.

Every person develops their own faculties and qualities. The Jewish people have developed the faculty of memory because of its long and ancient history. We remember the beginnings of our nation ... we start with the Bible, the five books of Moses; the creation of the world; our patriarchs, Abraham, Isaac and Jacob; our matriarchs, Sarah, Rebecca, Rachel, Leah; Moses; the Exodus from Egypt; and the destruction of our Temples, the Beit HaMikdash.

It is our duty to continue developing this memory and to include in it the Holocaust. It is our duty to tell and re-tell of our horrible experience to our children, grandchildren and friends. We have to teach it in schools, document it, write about it, tell it orally. Do NOT let it be forgotten! Already now 36 years after the Holocaust there are people bearing the title of professors who claim the Holocaust never happened, that it was a sheer Zionist propaganda.

We ask the question how it was possible that the German people, who produced scholars, writers and poets ... how

I visited the grave of our matriarch, Rachel, who was Jacob's wife, which is located, according to the Torah, "on the way to Efrata, which is Beit Lechem." This holy site is near Jerusalem.

could they have produced the most brutal beast in human history?

We hear from good friends when we speak about individuals or leaders of different states that threaten Israel with destruction. They say, don't take them seriously or they do it only for local reasons. And they have more reasons to justify this. Don't pay attention, they are crazy people! To these friends, we say there was one crazy man who said and wrote what he intended to do ... and people didn't take him seriously enough.

We must take seriously any threat against our existence ... any expression against any Jewish community in any part of the world because it is the crazy people who do not change their minds ... some people do change their minds ... they are more flexible. It is the mad person whom we must take seriously.

Writers, poets, survivors of the Holocaust ask themselves, "What is the answer to the Holocaust?" I don't think there is an answer to the Holocaust because the Holocaust itself is confronted with so many questions.

In the camps, we dreamed. Would we live? Would the day of freedom ever come?" That day did come, and that dream has become a reality.

I continue to dream. My recurring dream is that we continue to remind the world ... the world who would rather forget ... not to let another Holocaust happen to any human beings, Jews or non-Jews. Once is enough!

We Jews experienced something tragically historical that the outside world cannot relate to.

We represent survival. We represent endurance and perseverance. We overcame forces of evil and destruction.

I remember my arrival to Auschwitz, after three days in the boxcars, the SS in their long, leather coats, elegant, tall and clean shaven. I remember jumping out of the boxcar, already hungry and frightened. Then the line moved forward slowly until we came face-to-face with Dr. Mengele, the Angel of Death.

I was a young boy then ... I could not begin to image what was happening inside those gates. How can any human being imagine that in Auschwitz alone, a million of our brothers and sisters would be forced into a stark chamber ... naked ... and that they would be forced to breathe poison gas in agony until they were dead? How can you imagine that?! What did they do to deserve such cruel death?!

When I went through the gates of Auschwitz I wouldn't dare to dream that there would come a day thirty-six years later that people who survived this place would meet in Israel, in Jerusalem, the place promised by God.

Prime Minister Menachem Begin closed the historical meeting asking, "My brothers and sisters, how did it happen? How could it have happened in Europe in the twentieth century for six years? Not in a rage of a battle, but in the land of poets and philosophers as they called themselves ... turned into two-legged beasts of all evil in mankind? How could it have happened to our fathers and mothers ... brothers and sisters ... our sages ... some of the greatest in our history? To good-hearted people loving their families, devoted to their parents and children, God-fearing, believing in the coming of the Messiah and in redemption. And among them a million and a half of our children ... the children with their large, black eyes ... sad and loving eyes ... our sweethearts, our beloved ones?

Begin spoke about a question many people have asked ... "Should the Holocaust weaken our faith in God?" He said, "This question is a mistake. On the contrary, the Holocaust should strengthen our faith in God." He explained why the question where He was is not answerable by a mortal, but, were it not for Divine providence, everyone would have been annihilated.

Begin closed his speech saying, "There will never be a

repetition of the Holocaust as long as there is an Israel. No Jew will again be made to wear a yellow star or to be tattooed with a number. And I vow to you, there will forever be an Israel, so these horrors will never be witnessed again."

At one of the ceremonies, Elie Wiesel, a survivor from Buchenwald, who is a political activist and Nobel Laureate spoke of the oath for us to take.

This is what he said:

"We Take This Oath! We take it in the shadows of flames whose tongues scar the soul of our people. We vow in the name of dead parents and children; we vow, with our sadness hidden, our faith renewed; we vow we shall never let the sacred memory of our perished Six Million be scorned or erased.

We Saw Them: Hungry, in fear, we saw them rush to battle, we saw them in the loneliness of night ... true to their faith. At the threshold of death, we saw them. We received their silence in silence, merged their tears with ours.

Deportations, executions, mass-graves, death camps; mute prayers, cries of revolt, desperation, torn scrolls; cities and towns, villages and hamlets; the young, the old, the rich, the poor, ghetto fighters and partisans, scholars and messianic dreamers, ravaged faces, fists raised. Like clouds of fire, all have vanished.

We Take This Oath: Vision becomes word, to be handed down from father to son, from mother to daughter, from generation to generation.

Remember what the German killers and their accomplices did to our people. Remember them with rage and contempt. Remember what an indifferent world did to us and to itself. Remember the victims with pride and with sorrow. Remember also the deeds of the righteous Gentiles.

We Shall Also Remember: The miracle of the Jewish rebirth in the land of our ancestors, in the independent State of Israel. Here, pioneers and fighters returned to our people the dignity and majesty of nationhood. From the ruins of their lives, orphans and widows built homes and old-new fortresses on our redeemed land. To the end of our days we shall remember all those who realized and raised their dream ... our dream ... of redemption to the loftiest heights.

We Take This Oath: Here in Jerusalem, our eternal spiritual sanctuary. Let our legacy endure as a stone of the Temple Wall. For here prayers and memories burn. They burn and burn and will not be consumed."

Being a part of this gathering in Jerusalem, Israel, taking this oath, provides me with continued strength to remind you, the next generation ... never to forget!

לזכר נשמות

אביו ר' אברהם יצחק ב"ר משה ע"ה
נפטר א' תשרי תש"ה

אמו מרת הענטשע בת ר' יחיאל ע"ה
נפטרה ז' סיון תש"ד

אביה ר' נתן ב"ר אברהם ע"ה
נפטר ז' סיון תש"ד

אמה מרת לאה בת ר' ישעיה ע"ה
נפטרה ז' סיון תש"ד

וזכר נשמות הקדושים שנהרגו בשואה על קידוש השם

"זכור ואל תשכח"

ר' מאיר יהודה וייס ואשתו חוה

- -

Dedicated by
Mr. & Mrs. Michael Weiss
in memory of their parents
and in the memory of the Six Million Kedoshim
who perished in the Holocaust.

תנצב"ה

Heroes

When the German murderers and their helpers destroyed Kaszony and the surrounding communities, they destroyed the hopes and dreams and the potential creativity that the Jews could have contributed to the betterment of our society. I will never forget my family and friends, the victims, but also the heroes.

One such hero was Rabbi Chaim Michael Dov Weissmandl.

Rabbi Weissmandl.

He became known for his efforts to save the Jews by bribing German and Slovakian officials. He was successful in delaying the mass deportation of many Jews in my area for two years, from 1942 to 1944.

By bribing diplomats, Weissmandl was able to send out letters to people he hoped would help save the Jews of Europe, alerting them to the destruction of European Jewry. He managed to send letters to Winston Churchill and Franklin D. Roosevelt, and he had a diplomat deliver a letter to the Vatican.

He also begged the Allies to bomb the rails leading to Auschwitz, but to no avail.

"Drop bombs on the railroad tracks that lead to Auschwitz. Bomb the gas chambers and crematoriums. From the air the tracks are easily seen. Drop bombs on the bridges which lead from Hungary to Poland. Most of the people killed in Auschwitz are brought by rail, day and night. Every day thousands of Jews could be saved!"

Weissmandl was told that there are people in the gas chambers and they would be killed anyhow. The rabbi said,

"You can save the lives of so many people by destroying the chambers now though!" There was never a bomb dropped on the railroad tracks. It was never done because there were strict orders that there was to be no diversion of military force for the purpose of saving Jews.

Weissmandl believed that if the Hungarian Jews would resist, then only a small number of them would be deported, as the Germans in 1944 were already having difficulty enlisting enough soldiers to fight the war, and deal with the Jews at the same time.

Righteous Gentiles

We have all heard of the Gentiles who are recognized as "Righteous among the Nations." These non-Jews saved Jews, which proves that a single person or a few people could make a difference. There was the Swedish diplomat, Raoul Wallenberg, who distributed documents to thousands of Jews to stay in safehouses under the Swedish protection he set up in Budapest, Hungary.

I had my own experiences with the story of Mr. Wallenberg. After the war, I heard and read that there was a young Gentile man who finished his education at the University of Michigan and went back to Sweden. He became a diplomat in Hungary. He was sent to the counsel in Budapest. I read that he saved tens of thousands of Jews in Hungary and then I heard there was a young man whom Wallenberg saved. His name was Tom Lantos and he went to California and eventually became a representative from California in United States House of Representatives in Washington DC.

Tom Lantos came to Detroit, visited a religious school named Yeshiva Beth Yehudah where my son Mottel has been a rabbi and teacher for the last thirty years. I attended that gathering and we had a nice dinner.

After a very moving speech by the congressman, I shook

hands with him and he hugged me. I asked him if he could tell me something more about Mr. Wallenberg. He said, "Mr. Weiss, he saved 100,000 Hungarian Jews. We are proud of all the Gentiles who saved any Jews, to call them heroes of the Jewish people."

There were examples of courageous and righteous behavior in Amsterdam, although most of the people they tried to help were eventually caught and killed. There were approximately 25,000 Jews who were hidden at one time or another. Among them was the young Anne Frank and her family. The four people who chose to hide the Franks did so knowing they were endangering the lives of their family, yet they took the risk to offer assistance! This was not a simple act of moral conviction; it involved a painful decision-making process by jeopardizing family members.

Perhaps the most instructive history of rescue is the Danish one. Denmark was occupied by the Germans in 1940. In 1943, SS Headquarters in Berlin sent orders to the SS in Denmark demanding that all Jews in Denmark be rounded up for deportation to Auschwitz. The Danish Police and the Danish Civil Service refused to cooperate with the SS forces at that time. This was an amazingly brave and humanitarian stand. When the Germans went to round up the Jews of Denmark, the Danish population worked together to rescue over 7,000 Jews by sending them in boats to Sweden, where they were offered refuge. The Danes as a nation acted heroically.

In the small town of LeChambon, in southern France, the citizens hid Jews who managed to get there. The people of LeChambon then escorted the Jews during the night to Switzerland. The people of LeChambon, God bless them, as a group acted heroically.

There were many individuals who offered to hide Jews. Jews were hidden in every European city, Budapest, Paris and even in Berlin and other cities. In the rural areas of many countries, farmers hid Jews in their barns and cellars. Some clergymen hid Jews in churches and monasteries. Members of the underground prepared false identity papers for Jews. The people survived by hiding or running from one place to another. Like them, almost all who survived needed some help from someone at sometime.

The Danes, the people of LeChambon and all the people who did not stand with their eyes closed ... God allowed them to see the insanity of Hitler and The Third Reich. They proved that where there was a will to save Jews, God would show a way. Their value of human life made them "unwinged angels." Unfortunately, these angels were too few.

Today, as I complete this book, the Torah portion for the week is Va'yaira. There is a very important story here about a person who also struggled to save many people.

In this portion, Hashem walks with Abraham and says that He is going to destroy Sodom. Abraham questions Hashem about how many righteous people would need to be in the city in order for it not to be destroyed. From 50 righteous people down to 10, Hashem says He will not destroy the city. So this is my question. When the Nazis where murdering thousands and thousands of people every day, did Abraham beg or argue with Hashem to stop these murderers of His children?

Do Not Forget

My knowledge comes from my eyewitness experience in the Holocaust. As a survivor, I will remember this tragedy thrust upon the Jews of Europe and all the people murdered by the Nazis. These memories will remain with me forever.

It is the drive of the survivors that keeps their experiences in a time of the attempt to annihilate the Jewish people alive. We have to inspire our children, grandchildren, and the future generations to remember. The real tragedy would be to forget.

And to the deniers who try to lessen the Holocaust, I say, "I am here to tell the truth – in full!" This is one of the reasons that I continue to speak at the Holocaust center. I am an eyewitness to the Holocaust.

Do not forget the cities of slaughter or the gas chambers and crematoriums of Auschwitz, Treblinka and Buna or any other concentration camp. Remember the Warsaw Ghetto, the mass graves of Babi Yar and all the Jewish homes throughout Europe that were destroyed.

As long as survivors live, and as long as there will be democratic people, the survivors and their descendants cannot stop telling and retelling the facts related to the attempted destruction of the Jewish people. Just like I speak at the Holocaust center, the next generation has to continue speaking and keeping the account fresh. The moment the message becomes old and stale, it will be forgotten.

I do everything I can in order for the Holocaust to not be forgotten. My loss of family and friends is the main source for my commitment. From the depth of my heart, I strive to create an impact on my children and grandchildren, to create a living connection between my past and their future. They have to feel the pride in our heritage and make a commitment

The boxcar on exhibit at the Holocaust Center in Detroit.

to a continued dedication to keeping the remembrance alive.

Today, there is an original boxcar used by the Germans on exhibit at the Holocaust center in Detroit where I regularly speak about the Holocaust. When I walk by the boxcar on exhibit, I have to stop and look at it. I ask myself, "Could this be the cattle car I was locked in with my parents ... my family ... my friends ... my rabbi ... going to Auschwitz? During the transport, if memory serves me correctly, the boxcar stopped at some main stations. I think one of them was Kassa (or Kosice in Czech) and then it stopped in Krakow. From Krakow it continued to Auschwitz.

I have been a speaker for many years at the Holocaust Memorial Center Zekelman Family Campus in Detroit. We have about 80,000 visitors each year. After telling my experiences during the Holocaust, I encourage my audience to ask questions. Most of the time they are very interesting!

For example, I was asked, "Do you believe in God?" My answer was "I believe in God, no question about that!" My grandfather and grandmother, my father and mother ... and the generation before them, they all taught me to believe in

God. I believe that God is our father. A child can ask, 'Father, what happened?' And even ask why it happened."

Then another memorable question I was asked by a teenaged girl, about five years ago, "Can there be another Holocaust for the Jewish people?" To tell you the truth, I didn't expect that question! So thoughtful ... so smart. To me that meant that this young lady was listening to what I said! I told her, "I don't think there will be another Holocaust for us Jews." If you ask me today though, I'm not so sure. Anti-Semitism is rampant throughout Europe again, in the same countries where it happened in the 1930s and 1940s.

In Hungary, recent research shows today, June 20, 2015, the percentage of hardcore anti-Semites in Hungary has more than doubled in the past two decades to somewhere between to 21-28% of the population. Nearly one-third of the Hungarians believe anti-Jew conspiracy theories such as "Jews seek to rule the world."

Oh please God help us ... I heard this just before we were forced out of our home to the ghetto and taken to Auschwitz.

Events For Remembering

In the Jewish calendar we have a number of national days when we remember our past.

On Passover, we recall the cruel slavery of the Israelites in Egypt and the exodus from slavery to freedom.

On Tisha B'Av, we recall the destruction of both Temples in Jerusalem and the loss of statehood.

On Chanukah, we remember the struggle of the Maccabees against religious oppression.

On Purim, we remember the great danger the Jews of Persia experienced and the triumph over Haman.

On "Yom HaShoah," the day set aside to reflect and remember the Holocaust, we recall the tragedy that befell our people in Europe at the hands of the most inhumane and powerful regimes the Jewish people ever encountered. In Israel, at 10 a.m., a siren sounds throughout the country. Everyone stops what they are doing, and stands to remember. Even the cars on the highways come to a full stop, and the drivers get out and stand safely during the minutes of the siren.

On February 26, 2004, a Holocaust Bill was signed into law by Michigan Governor Jennifer Granholm. The law was signed to remember and commemorate one of the darkest periods of world history. The law designates the 27th day of the Hebrew month of Nisan, which falls in April-May, as Holocaust Remembrance Day in Michigan. The entire week is used in observing and remembering the Holocaust. Representative Marc Shulman, R-West Bloomfield, the bill's sponsor, said, "This remembrance of the Holocaust is more than a history lesson; it is a current event." My wife and I had the privilege to join Representative Shulman and Lt. Gov. John Cherry at the signing of this historic law.

Compared to the thousands of years that Jews lived in

Governor Rick Snyder, myself, Senator Debbie Stabenow, Senator Carl Levin. Taken at the dinner of Yeshiva Beth Yehuda.

Europe and contributed greatly to its growth, the cruel murderers, in just a short few years, destroyed it all. The once beautiful land became blood-soaked. It became a cursed land.

Now, seventy years after the Holocaust, the smell still lingers. I cannot forget what happened in Auschwitz or Buchenwald. I cannot forgive the perpetrators of the Holocaust for what they did to all those who died at their hands..

I shall never forget as my family, my congregation and my rabbi and I were herded into the boxcars to be taken to Auschwitz. The people in the boxcars were saying, "as soon as America finds out what is going on, she will surely stop this." That is the kind of faith we the Jewish people of Europe had in America, who was known throughout Europe until then as the protector of those in distress.

But we, the survivors, who love America very much, have difficulty with some of the things that happened during that period. In the time of our need, America didn't act to save

Nikolsburger Rebbe and myself.

the Jews during the Holocaust. President Roosevelt and his government were bystanders. Roosevelt was very much interested in the idea of settling the Jews of Europe in a remote place like Madagascar in the Indian Ocean, since this would have served the British well.

We Jews respect the pope very well. We respect his religion, but we shouldn't forget that the powerful Catholic Church and its spiritual leader Pope Pious XII, with his moral authority, remained silent all those years, although he received many appeals from non-Jewish and Jewish leaders like the chief rabbi of Israel, Rabbi Hertzog. They appealed to him to speak out against the atrocities.

We'd like to think that one remark from the pope to his followers would have saved countless Jews. Even some Nazis might have reconsidered their action, but he remained silent.

The International Red Cross knew about the condition in the labor camps, concentration camps and death camps. However, their official policy was to not reveal the horrors and crimes the Germans and their collaborators were committing during the Second World War. The International Red Cross didn't attempt to arouse public opinion against the daily crimes which were committed against the Jews. The International Red Cross admitted a few years ago that they could have done more, and could have been more aggressive in their responsibilities.

There were hungry Jewish prisoners in the concentration camps who witnessed the distribution of life-saving food parcels to all camp inmates except Jews. The parcels were clearly marked in bold letters that the packages were for the prisoners from the International Red Cross. The International Red Cross said they were following German orders to exclude Jews as recipients.

Even now, I am not able to contribute to the Red Cross. I still remember that I couldn't taste the precious food in those parcels we so needed.

The Adolf Eichmann trial in Jerusalem, Israel in 1961 presented to the world a broader picture of the tragedy of the great losses of the Jewish people during the Holocaust.

The German murderers were not robots. They were men and women who were made into a killing machine.

The combination and Nazi ideology and advanced technology to carry out the genocide of European Jewry characterize the Holocaust. The fact that a society could be so overtaken, like the Germans were, must serve as reminder to the human race of the danger which stems from hatred, based on ideology and religion, and the destruction of human values and morality. We already see this fanaticism returning in the ideologies of the democratic enemies of the Middle East.

Tisha B'Av And The Holocaust

The Hebrew month of Av is a month of mourning for the Jewish people. On Tisha B'Av, the ninth day of Av, we remember the many tragedies that had befallen our people. We mourn the destruction of the first and second Temples that were destroyed over two thousand years ago. Tens of thousands of men and women were killed by the Romans just because they were Jewish. We were driven out from our holy country that God Himself gave to us.

On Tisha B'Av we must also add the Holocaust to the list of tragedies for which the Jewish people must mourn.

Throughout this book, I write how the Nazis destroyed everything holy and dear to us. I remind you that they murdered six million of our dearest possessions ... our fathers, mothers and families, of which one and a half million were children.

In Hebrew, the Holocaust is called "Shoah." The martyrs are remembered as the "Kedoshim."

Everyone is obligated to remember the Holocaust, not just those who survived, or who have a direct family connection to the martyrs. In reality, all Jews have a direct connection to the six million Kedoshim and just like we remember the destruction of our Temples, we must remember the destruction of Europe. God forbid if people forget them ... that would make Hitler the victor.

Hashem, know that we have sinned, but we are still Your children. Have "rachmanus" on Your children. Grant us "Geula Shelema Bimhayra Beyamaenu" (that we should see the real redemption in our time).

Kinot (Sad Poetry) To Remember Tisha B'Av

Oh how thou hast cast down our glory from our head,
Oh how thou hast hidden thyself from us,
Oh how thou wast angry and has no pity.

With a broken and contrite heart, on a day of fasting and
convocation,
We come before thee, to mourn and weep with deep
lamentation,
When we recall the Martyrs of the 1939-45 European
devastation.

Thou hast crushed the pride of Jacob,
whom thou didst love,
Thou hast cut off the lofty of stature,
and degraded the tall ones,
Thou hast laid waste our vines,
and blighted our fig trees ... the pleasant and the beloved,
the upright and the perfect ones,
Loaded onto the wagons ... like sheep and cattle.
The heat was suffocating, the doors were sealed.

Distinguished scholars sit on the ground in stunned silence,
"What, Oh what, was their guilt?" they ask.
And why was the decree issued without mercy?

Heads of families, mighty men of valor,
Millions fell slain and wounded,
It was a disgrace and a horror for the nations.

They went down alive into the nether-world saying "Shema
Yisrael" and singing "Ani-Maamin."

Their souls departed while they were wrapped
in Tallit and Tefillin,
Let the murderers be put to shame and confusion,
and be as naught.

Our flesh and our hearts fail at the destruction of half of
our nation,
For the European Holocaust ranks equal to the
destruction of our Temple.
To Auschwitz, Buchenwald, Bergen-Belsen, Dachau,
Medanek and Treblinka,
Where they were taken in disgrace, thrust into the Gas-
chambers, and burned in the furnaces,
Yet in the Warsaw Ghetto, the holy martyrs fought, and
fell like warriors.

From every corner their congealed blood cries out,
"Oh when will the end come to the severe afflictions?"
Take up bitter lamentation and wailing
for the holy martyrs!

Our eyes shed tears
For the burning of Synagogues,
For the destruction of Yeshivot and Academies.
They destroyed our assemblies,
and demolished our congregations,

Fear came upon us, and trembling seized us,
In our distress confusion was heard as far as the Red Sea.

Our kinsfolk and dearly loved friends,
Pious and upright,
Holy and pure,
Shining as brightness of the firmament,
Receive and shelter them forever
Under the cover of thy wings.

Oh Merciful One!
Remember in thy mercy the remnants of thy heritage,
Sovereign of the universe!
Remove anxiety and grief from thy people.

Uproot in thy wrath the wickedness of the nations and
the enemies of Israel.

Proclaim liberty to the captives,
and release our prisoners.
Crown us with the oil of joy, in place of mourning.
Grant peace and tranquility to us and to our land.

Raise our power and hasten our redemption,
speedily in our days.

Let Israel our State blossom like a rose,
Oh Merciful One,
Bless us with the blessing vouchsafed to
Abraham, Isaac, and Jacob.

The Talmud teaches in Tractate Sanhedrin –

Whoever destroys a single life is as guilty as though he destroyed the entire world.

And

Whoever saves a single life is thought of as if he had saved an entire world.

Six Million Lives Destroyed.

Six Million Worlds Never To Be.

Our generation of Jews has experienced the greatest loss ever.

Always Remember!

Made in the USA
Columbia, SC
08 July 2021

41570708R00074